Praise for So Brightly at the Last

A terrific book. I read it with astonishment and learnt a huge amount. It's informal, enthusiastic, chatty and leaves the reader in no doubt about Clive's formidable scope and range.

PROFESSOR JOHN CAREY

A lively, unpredictable guide to Clive James's late work. Anyone interested in his astonishing career will want to read this book.

CHRISTIAN WIMAN

Clive James is possibly the greatest prose stylist of his generation; erudite, elegant, funny and penetrating. All that, though, applies equally to his poetry, less well known but just as dazzling. Shircore's book is a long overdue, very readable but insightful celebration of James's wonderful and humane lyric verse.

STUART MACONIE

A fascinating study of Clive James's lifelong dedication to poetry—a compelling portrait of the man through the work. Not to be missed.

STEPHEN EDGAR

Ian Shircore has given Clive's poetry the care and attention it richly deserves. This is a sensitive treatment of a body of poetry that has flourished so beautifully near the end.

PHILIP COLLINS

Clive James's verse is alive with energy, wit. craft, beauty, fire and a uniquely thrilling poetic intelligence.

STEPHEN FRY

Praise for Loose Canon: the Extraordinary Songs of Clive James and Pete Atkin

'I loved this book, right from Stephen Fry's gorgeous introduction...
I especially recommend this to folks who don't know the songs... I envy
anyone hearing them for the first time'

'Written beautifully'

'A brilliant book about one of the greatest, but least well known,
songwriting partnerships of the last 100 years'

'I read this book in one sitting, it's that readable and engaging'

'An essential read'

'Thoroughly enjoyable both for dipping in and for longer sessions...even
for those who don't really know them yet, it's definitely worth a punt'

'It is rare you find a book where the written narrative is as lyrical as the
songs themselves, but *Loose Canon* is one of those books'

'A beautifully written exploration of the songs of Clive James and
Pete Atkin...there's no better way of understanding them more clearly,
and appreciating them more deeply'

'This book should be of interest to anyone interested
in the craft of songwriting'

'If you're a fan it's a must and if you're not...well, you're missing a treat!!'

'A fabulously well researched and entertaining read'

'Cracking read. I knew next to nothing about James/Atkin and their work
but was drawn into the story from the first chapter'

'I loved this book. It's well written, illuminating, full of humour and a real
joy to read. Ian Shircore is an excellent writer and this is his best book yet'

'What an enjoyable, interesting read, filled with some beautiful
and touching moments'

CLIVE JAMES

AND THE PASSION FOR POETRY

SO BRIGHTLY
AT THE LAST

IAN SHIRCORE

Red Door

Published by RedDoor

www.reddoorpress.co.uk

© 2019 Ian Shircore

ISBN 978-1-913062-07-1

Typesetting: Tutis Innovative E-Solutions Pte. Ltd

Print and production handled by Jellyfish Solutions Ltd

This book is for Zoë and Nick, the great-great-grandchildren of Eleanor Parkman, whose grandma heard the news of Waterloo as it happened, and for Clive, whose words have been precious to me for half a century

Contents

1

You Can't Expect to Be Remembered

For half a lifetime, Clive James has lived with fear. It's not the fear of death. That's a done deal, so there's no point fretting about it. 'Stop worrying. No-one gets out of here alive,' he says. What does worry him is the dread suspicion that the obituaries, when they eventually come, will fail to give him credit for any of his achievements in the fields of literature, music and cultural criticism, including forty books, two hundred song lyrics and fifty years of dedicated devotion to the poetic muse.

Instead, they will focus, he fears, on the other side of his public role. He has seen the headlines in his dreams: 'Japanese game show man dies.'

That would be a harsh reward for a long and dazzling career that has seen Clive hailed as the most versatile writer of his generation. No-one who's relished his exuberant, provocative TV and literary criticism should ever forget that he invented a new way of writing about such things – a way that's so firmly established it's become today's orthodoxy. No-one who has enjoyed his million-selling *Unreliable Memoirs* can question his ability to create moments of comic genius. No-one who has read *Cultural Amnesia*, his vast survey of the words, wars, music, people and politics that shaped the twentieth century, could doubt his erudition, his wit or his serious engagement with the greatest issues of our time. And no-one who has read recent works like 'Japanese Maple' or his book-length poem, *The River in the Sky*, could fail to recognise the late flowering that has finally confirmed his status as a genuinely talented poet.

But who wants someone who's a poet, essayist, comedian and critic – and, of course, television presenter – all rolled into one?

It confuses people. It makes it hard to know what to expect. When a critic from *The New Yorker*, back in the last century, declared 'Clive James is a brilliant bunch of guys', he deftly summed up both the strengths and weaknesses of Clive's unique and ambiguous position in our culture. He is today's Renaissance Man. But, as he pointed out years ago, in an essay on Pier Paolo Pasolini, that's a tag that has been devalued by overuse.

'Renaissance Man is a description tossed around too lightly in modern times,' he observed, striking his best Noël Coward pose. 'Actors get it if they can play the guitar.'

The 'Japanese game show man' label is part of the picture. For millions, Clive will always be the amiable Aussie with the hooded, piercing eyes and the wry Cheshire Cat grin who entertained them for twenty years with shows like *Saturday Night Clive*, the *Postcard From...* travel documentaries and *Clive James on Television*. When this last series unearthed the spectacularly brutal Japanese 'torture TV' game show *Za Gaman* – otherwise known as *Endurance* – British television crossed a watershed.

We had never seen reality TV before, except for the rather more sedate *Candid Camera*. We gasped at the humiliating trials contestants were put through and told ourselves it could never happen here. It never has, quite, but it didn't take us long to get used to seeing our own minor celebrities tucking into a meal of roast spider or grilled crocodile penis and being showered with glistening cockroaches.

Alongside this television stardom, Clive was still producing thoughtful, incisive essays and literary criticism, still adding volumes to his *Unreliable Memoirs* and still writing poetry. Occasionally, a poem of his would cut through the hubbub and make its mark in the outside world. His splendidly spiteful 'The Book of My Enemy Has Been Remaindered' dates from the early eighties, but it is still being shared with glee across today's social media. It may, even now, prove to be his most long-lasting poem, if only because it has three decades' start on the remarkable surge of work he has produced since he became seriously ill, nine years ago.

People come to Clive James by a variety of different routes. I first knew him as a songwriter, the lyricist who worked with singer Pete Atkin in the early seventies. I didn't know he wrote poetry then, but I was well aware of a sneaky poetic tendency in the words he wrote for their largely humorous songs.

One of the first I heard was called 'You Can't Expect to Be Remembered', a little ditty that warned modern lovers that they couldn't hope to be immortalised in 'balanced lapidary phrases' like those so casually knocked out, in days of yore, by the likes of Petrarch, Shakespeare and Ronsard. These bards of old, the song explained, couldn't put pen to paper without creating works of enduring genius. You could scarcely fail to notice Clive's nonchalant hijacking of one of the great lines from Shakespeare's Sonnet 18 ('They never said "Farewell", they said "So long" / "So long lives this and this gives life to thee"'), introduced by the splendidly anachronistic and slangy 'So long'. I loved this stuff. It was funny. It was smart. It certainly wasn't the sort of thing you stumbled across every day in the folk clubs and student bars of 1970s Britain.

This song and other gems on Pete's first album, *Beware of the Beautiful Stranger* – including 'Touch Has a Memory', which was based on a line from Keats, and 'Have You Got a Biro I Can Borrow?', which wasn't – opened my eyes to Clive's playful, quirky way of looking at the world and my ears to his unique way with words. I moved on to enjoy his TV criticism in the *Observer* and, eventually, his long mock-heroic satire of mid-seventies literary London, *Peregrine Prykke's Pilgrimage*. By the time he started to appear regularly on television, I was hungry for just about anything he came up with. I've been a fan ever since. It hasn't always been an uncritical acceptance – there's a grain of truth in his friend Frederic Raphael's sly comment that 'Clive's written too much' – but I've always found there's something to savour, even in his least successful efforts. And his gradual emergence as a poet of acknowledged stature has been a joy to watch.

Clive has always wanted to be taken seriously, to be judged on the quality of his work, rather than on his jokey public persona. When we were talking, at his home in Cambridge, after the publication of *Loose Canon*, my book about his songwriting career, I suddenly

4

realised that no-one had attempted a proper critical assessment of his poetry. Given the slightest encouragement – which he generously provided – I felt that I should take on the task, if only to ensure that something of the sort had been done before his failing health took him away from us.

* * *

This book will surprise you. If you are not aware that this learned, cerebral man spent ten weeks locked up in a closed ward at a mental hospital during the early stages of his long final illness ('With the Trouser Thief and the lady with one song / She sang for ever', as his poem 'Recollected in Tranquillity' tells us), it may even shock you.

If you think of Clive James mainly as a cynical, wisecracking phrasemaker, you may be surprised at the depth and intensity of his poetry, from 'At Ian Hamilton's Funeral' (written in 2002) right through to 'Injury Time' and his last long (and mostly unrhymed) autobiographical poem, *The River in the Sky*, published in late 2018. You may be unexpectedly moved by his devastating poem about Asma al-Assad, wife of Syria's murderous dictator, and startled by the rabid ferocity of some of his detractors – most of them Australian – who see him as a windbag charlatan, constantly engaged in perpetrating poetic con tricks that only they can see through.

Clive has always been a Marmite character, dividing opinion and provoking strong reactions, for and against. But those who line up on his side of the argument know that he gives them special pleasures. He is clever, well-read (in eight languages, including Russian and Japanese) and genuinely enthusiastic about the arts –

highbrow, lowbrow and everything in between, from Marvell and Auden, Rembrandt and Beethoven to *The Sopranos*, *Game of Thrones*, 'Hit Me With Your Rhythm Stick' and 'Jailhouse Rock'. Alongside his vivid and explosive way with words, it's this generous enthusiasm, the boyish urge to discover what's admirable and share it with his readers, that makes his writing so enjoyable. For fifty years, in prose and poetry, he has brought us the fruits of his explorations, dropping them happily at our feet the way a proud puppy lays half a squirrel in loving tribute on your kitchen floor.

The insights and discoveries come in all shapes and sizes. You'll find them scattered through the poems featured in this book. But they are everywhere in Clive's poetry, popping up in many of the minor poems and verse letters I have not mentioned here. You don't need to know the context to be stopped in your tracks by a line like 'Men who burn books burn men' (from a rambling poem written on the occasion of his honorary degree ceremony at the University of Sydney). The same piece includes a deft definition of the scope of Clive's own talents ('My territory's the chattering hedgerow / Between the neat fields forming the landscape / Of proper scholarship'), though much of the rest of the poem is eminently forgettable. The same applies to his verse letter 'To Craig Raine: A Letter from Biarritz', which is uncomfortably salacious in places, yet still yields some fine lines about the validity of cheap verbal thrills: 'But on the whole there's some cause to be proud / If what you write makes people laugh aloud' and 'A joke's a joke and it needs no excuse'.

The most extreme example of this patchy glory is his poem about the now-disgraced artist and entertainer Rolf Harris, which was quietly dropped from 2016's *Collected Poems*. Harris was originally a swimmer, a backstroke expert and Australian junior champion. Writing in 2000 about the backstroker's curious view of the world, Clive points out that these swimmers are isolated figures who 'must get used to being on their own'.

Like the Aymara-speaking peoples of Bolivia and Peru, whose metaphors for time position the past in front of them and the future out of sight behind their backs, the backstroke swimmers have a different view of the world from most of us: 'Backstrokers squint to ward off the bright sky / And at the most they see where they have been. / His future lay behind him.' It's an interesting idea, even though, in view of Harris's subsequent convictions for historical sex offences, it is now coloured with a deep shade of irony.

Clive's recent poems are more surefooted. His later works, apart from 2018's epic *The River in the Sky*, have been shorter. Like the earlier poems, they are studded with wonderfully inventive turns of phrase, offbeat ideas and unexpected associations and connections. One of the best poems from his 2013 collection, *Nefertiti in the Flak Tower*, draws a parallel between his friend Peter Porter's death and the hushed and empty skies caused by the Icelandic volcano of 2010. Another likens cancer ward patients ('bare-arsed warriors' he calls them, 'dressed to strike fear into the enemy') to paratroopers waiting for the drop into dangerous territory. It begins:

> Taking the piss out of my catheter,
> The near-full plastic bag bulks on my calf
> As I drag my I.V. tower through Addenbrooke's

Like an Airborne soldier heading for D-Day
Down the longest corridor in England.

A third, 'The Falcon Growing Old', is full of gem-like phrases. The ageing bird, 'the poised assassin', streaking effortlessly down, 'scarcely moves a muscle as it rides / A silent avalanche back to the wrist', drawing on a lifetime's practice and experience as a substitute for youthful effort. The ageing writer, hoping for the same success, must trust his own hard-won skills to bring his poem down in a long glide to the rendezvous point, 'a dead heat with your shadow'.

What's different about these poems and those that followed, in *Sentenced to Life* (2015) and *Injury Time* (2017), is that Clive's strike rate has improved. Frail and battered, distracted only by frequent routine or blue-light trips to the hospital, he has come to focus almost exclusively on the key issues of illness, family and his approaching death. His renowned ability to 'turn a phrase until it catches the light' hasn't necessarily improved, but his discipline has. The later poems are less hit-and-miss. And he knows it.

'I think the control I had over my work was less than adequate,' he says. 'There was nothing wrong with the good bits in my poems. It's just that they were packed around with lots and lots of bad bits. The only way I've improved in the last several decades is that I've learned to leave out the bad bits. I'm not sure you do improve beyond that.'

The Japanese game show man has come a long way. The memory of his television work is slow to fade, even after nearly two decades, and it's quite possible that his much-misquoted quip about Arnold

Schwarzenegger's muscled body looking 'like a brown condom full of walnuts' will still reverberate long after both Clive and Arnie have left us.

But he's got his wish. Clive James has made his mark. There is a general acceptance these days that his later work has secured his place as a poet of considerable power and range. As he wrote, prophetically, in the last verse of 'Japanese Maple':

> A final flood of colours will live on
> As my mind dies,
> Burned by my vision of a world that shone
> So brightly at the last, and then was gone.

2

The Price of Fame

The problem was television. People forget that television – other than live football, *Strictly* and a few other event-based shows – is writing, too. Clive has always been a writer and he's always operated on the premise that his first duty is to grab and hold an audience: 'I work on the assumption that the reader will stop reading if I stop being interesting.'

In the interests of interestingness, his shows were opinionated, often superficial, sometimes bordering on the xenophobic, frequently inclined to go for the cheap laugh. If they were too knowing, though, it was because Clive always knew what he was trying to do.

He understood television, its magnetism and its limitations. His much-quoted dictum, 'Anyone afraid of what he thinks television does to the world is probably just afraid of the world', encapsulated one aspect of this understanding. His less familiar belief that 'Television is just your eyes and ears on a stalk' was equally important in informing his activities.

But Clive's TV output was not all pure entertainment. The majestic 1993 series *Fame in the 20th Century* was a thrilling, accessible and often amusing tour de force – a crash course in history and the humanities, showing how the arrival of sound recording, moving pictures, and, crucially, the close-up, had changed the nature of fame for ever. The eight-part series pulled in clips of more than 250 highlights and cameos of twentieth-century life, from the Wright brothers' first plane staggering into the air at Kitty Hawk in 1903 to Trump and Pavarotti, Princess Di and Madonna, Salman Rushdie and Saddam Hussein in the early nineties. Alongside historic newsreel sequences and classic moments from the silver screen, Clive's tireless researchers had discovered all kinds of unexpected treasures, such as the only surviving film of Queen Victoria and twenty-two flickering seconds of Tolstoy and his beard walking along a railway platform. They had also dug up some revealing footage of political leaders, such as the brief glimpse of Roosevelt struggling to limp a few yards on his polio-damaged legs, and both Adolf Hitler and Idi Amin hamming it up for the cameras in their own home movies.

The main thesis – that the twentieth century first created the mechanism for global fame and then handed power to those who used it most effectively – was persuasively argued in Clive's carefully written script. During WWI, the international reach of the silent movie made Charlie Chaplin the most famous person in the world. Between the wars, it was Johnny Weissmuller, then Walt Disney, then Greta Garbo. By the late 1930s, it was Hitler, who seemed unstoppable until he came up against the equally image-conscious Churchill. After the war, the emphasis shifted back to entertainment and sport (with the rise of television stars like Lucille Ball and Liberace, followed by Elvis, The Beatles and Muhammad Ali) until

Ronald Reagan finally brought the two strands of showbiz and politics together in the White House.

Fame in the 20th Century was an international co-production, mainly funded by the BBC's licence payers. Two years in the making, it was shown four times on PBS in America and twice in Australia, but it had just one midweek outing on the BBC, on Wednesday nights, despite its huge cost and an audience of five to seven million viewers. Restrictive licensing arrangements for the hundreds of clips meant the cost of reshowing the series would have been prohibitive and it sank virtually without trace (though all the shows, except for Episode 8, can now be seen on YouTube, at least until someone notices they are there).

The book of the series – sharp, readable and closely based on the original script – remains a favourite for many Clive James fans. It touches on several of the same themes as his masterwork, *Cultural Amnesia*, including what Clive calls 'the big story of modern times, the long conflict between democracy and totalitarianism'. But the requirements of chronological sequencing and television scripting mean the stories, insights and jokes are packed into short, direct sentences that carry it along at a breathtaking pace. Even without the pictures to back it up, the commentary sings and fizzes with life. Twenty years after the paperback went out of print, it must surely be time for Penguin and the BBC to consider a new edition.

Fame in the 20th Century was the pinnacle of Clive's television career, but it is not what people remember him for. His constant on-screen presence over two decades created the lasting impression of an entertainer, rather than a film-maker and, inevitably, influenced the reaction to his poetry. Those who knew he had so much more to offer never stopped clucking over his willingness to embrace his TV role. But, as he has often pointed out, it was only his fame that gave him access to a wider public.

'I believe in mass communication, not art for the few,' he says. 'The short answer to why I am wasting my talent is that I never heard much about this talent before I started wasting it.'

And there were certain more mundane things to worry about, like earning a living. Clive had learned to savour the finer things in life, when they were available, but his demands were modest. When he went on tour with his musical partner, Pete Atkin, he was always perfectly content with the Spartan comforts of the nearest Travelodge ('A bed, a shower and a desk to write on – what else do you need?'). But poetry, as a career, fell far short of offering the kind of financial security needed to support his wife, Prue, a brilliant but underpaid Italian scholar, and two growing daughters. Artistic ambition was tempered with pragmatic realism.

'Television paid for the groceries,' he says now. 'As a poet, I'd have starved.'

Throughout his years on the small screen, Clive was always writing poetry. He had sold his time, but not his soul. Whatever the public and the commentators thought of him, he still saw himself as a practising poet with real ambitions to produce well-crafted work that would be enjoyed by an audience beyond the tiny cluster of poets, critics, publishers and academics who make up the poetry industry.

Several of the poems he wrote during this period – including 'Johnny Weissmuller Dead in Acapulco', 'Six Degrees of Separation from Shelley', 'Dream Me Some Happiness' and 'The Lions at Taronga' – showed impressive technical facility and scope. They also demonstrated some of Clive's trademark techniques, such as his habit of creating verses that are ostensibly based on well-known personalities, stories or locations but eventually circle round to reveal an unexpectedly personal, autobiographical element. Though most of them passed relatively unnoticed at the time, they have held up well and chart his steady progress towards a new poetic maturity.

Not everything he wrote was accepted for print, but he did manage to get many of his shorter poems published by some very respectable and discriminating literary journals. And, now and again, something would break through and remind the wider public that the glib television image was not the whole story.

In 1983, for example, the august *London Review of Books* featured a new poem, 'The Book of My Enemy Has Been Remaindered', which is still a major landmark in Clive's career. Over the years, it has found a place in many anthologies, and it is still retweeted every week or two, with obvious delight, by a new generation of readers who clearly regard it as something more than a thirty-six-year-old period piece.

It has also attracted some unexpected fans, including Australia's Liberal Party prime minister, Malcolm Turnbull.

'I have seen it reported that he quotes "The Book of My Enemy Has Been Remaindered" at dinner parties,' Clive told a startled interviewer from the *Australian* newspaper. 'I therefore judge him to be the greatest democratic politician since Pericles.'

'The Book of My Enemy' is a masterpiece of well-honed schadenfreude, a hilarious, malicious, crowing, vindictive and irresistibly sadistic hymn to the sheer joy of witnessing a literary rival's humiliation. Its enduring appeal stems partly from its subject matter, partly from its vibrant energy and gusto and partly from an attention to detail in its execution that is easily underestimated by the casual reader.

Structurally, 'The Book of My Enemy' is less formless than it seems at first glance. The four apparently amorphous stanzas are all roughly sonnet-sized, alternating between fifteen and thirteen lines, and though there is nothing resembling an organised rhyme scheme, this is unmistakably something more than prose. The opening stanza announces itself as poetry with a brief feint in the direction of ABAB formality ('remaindered', 'pleased', 'remaindered', 'seized') and the rhyming of 'piles' and 'aisles' in the sixth and eighth lines. But although unobtrusive and widely spaced rhymes do occur later on ('rejoice' and 'voice' in the second stanza, 'one' and 'fun' towards the end of the third), it soon becomes clear that we are not in Kipling territory. Nor should we expect the metrical reassurance of steady iambic pentameters. The familiar devices of poetic technique – assonance, alliteration ('posturing and pretence', closely followed by '*Pertwee's Promenades and Pierrots*') and half-rhymes ('wrapper' and 'skyscraper') – all play their part in contributing to the texture of the verses, but their presence could almost be coincidental. What gives the poem its unity is its loose but insistent speech-based rhythm, combined with an unusual and specific tone of voice.

The opening line, for example, has a scriptural, psalm-like ring, and a lot of the fun derives from the interplay between the many echoes of the King James Bible and the slangy modernity of phrases like 'complete stiffs' or 'The bummers that no amount of hype could shift'.

15

The protagonist has seen his enemy, the fashionable literary Goliath with his awards and prizes and his 'delicate, quivering sensibility', downed and disgraced, and his cup runneth over with churlish glee.

The archaic phrasing runs right through the poem, from the 'behold' in the first stanza and 'beneath the yoke' and 'what avail him now' in the second to the 'yea' in the third and the Old Testament 'chastisement' in the last verse. Simply by setting up these glaring contrasts between the sanctimonious language of the psalmist and the racy vernacular of the sneering narrator, Clive has invested the poem with a seductively mock-heroic quality. None of us, of course, would take such cruel and indecent pleasure in a colleague's misfortune. But which of us can honestly say that we haven't felt a twitch of delight at seeing an enemy come a cropper? Our identification with the narrator does us no credit at all, but it's not something we can help.

Clive claims that 'The Book of My Enemy' was prompted by an actual experience of seeing a rival's work stacked waist-high among the remaindered dross, though he has always refused to name names.

'It was almost a religious experience,' he says. 'It's a sin to rejoice so much in someone else's misfortune, to write out of vengefulness. But I did see these huge piles of deservedly unsold books. And I did enjoy it. It wasn't my most worthy moment, but I probably had more fun writing this poem than anything else I ever wrote.'

This is a duel between two direct competitors, jostling for a seat at literature's top table and keen to establish their moral and intellectual credentials for this exalted status. The loser's 'slim volume with its understated wrapper', his 'sensibility and its hair-like filaments' and 'His honesty, proclaimed by himself and believed in by others, / His

16

renowned abhorrence of all posturing and pretence' are all part of this carefully orchestrated image-building – and thus are suitable targets for the narrator's corrosive scorn. The enemy has been praised for his 'meticulous technique' and 'unmistakably individual new voice'. But this shower of reviewer's clichés generates some wonderful contrasts with the flashy tawdriness of the remaindered books.

The slim volume 'consorts with the bad buys, / The sinkers, clinkers, dogs and dregs'. It wallows among 'the Edsels of the world of movable type' – a reference to the Ford Edsel (1957), which has gone down in history as the worst and most overhyped car ever made. It 'bathes in the glare of the brightly jacketed *Hitler's War Machine*' and sits alongside *The Kung-Fu Cookbook* and *Pertwee's Promenades and Pierrots: One Hundred Years of Seaside Entertainment*. But the most degrading association of all is with *Barbara Windsor's Book of Boobs*, with its alluring cover line 'My boobs will give everyone hours of fun'.

The cumulative impact of these four ridiculous titles is devastating and richly comic. But, in fact, only one of them is Clive's own imaginative contribution. The other three all exist, and can still be ordered online, should anyone want them. *Hitler's War Machine* was published by Hamlyn in 1976. *Pertwee's Promenades and Pierrots: One Hundred Years of Seaside Entertainment*, written by Bill Pertwee, who played Air Raid Warden Hodges in *Dad's Army*, came out in 1979. And so, too, did *Barbara Windsor's Book of Boobs*, complete with the 'hours of fun' come-on line that's faithfully recorded in the poem. The odd one out – Clive's inspired creation, *The Kung-Fu Cookbook* – is an idea that has never been taken up, though DreamWorks did produce *The Kung-Fu Panda 2 Interactive Cookbook* for children a few years ago.

And, of course, it goes without saying that if any of the narrator's own works should ever, by some mischance, end up in this little shop of literary horrors, it will be for quite different reasons: 'a miscalculated print run, a marketing error – / Nothing to do with merit'.

Although Clive is happy to play the gloating pantomime villain in this poem, the edgy rivalries among the members of London's incestuous literary elite in the seventies and eighties were hardly a secret. Backs were certainly scratched, but plenty were stabbed as well. Despite the ties of friendship, many of Clive's colleagues were very happy to take him down a peg when the opportunity arose to review his poetry. The scrupulously exacting editor, critic and poet Ian Hamilton, a man Clive loved and admired and who was his companion through many gruelling four-hour lunchtimes in the pubs and restaurants of Soho, was especially ruthless in his condemnation of his friend's flaws and vanities, as well as his writing. Reviewing the fourth – and weakest – of Clive's mock-heroic sagas, the overblown and over-hyped *Charles Charming's Challenges on the Pathway to the Throne*, Hamilton handed out a brisk and unstinting dose of tough love.

The *Sunday Times* had already awarded this epic the title of 'Worst Poem of the Twentieth Century'. Hamilton quoted this line gleefully in his review, before going on to call *Charles Charming* pointless, 'pale and laborious' and 'squirm-inducing'. In retrospect, Clive agrees. He calls it 'my single biggest catastrophe' and says it 'put a hole in my reputation that took in water for the next thirty years'.

But it wasn't just the text of the poem that came under fire. It was also Clive's personal weaknesses – what Hamilton saw as his fawning courtier's unwillingness to go for the throat, coupled with his strenuously feeble efforts to appear tough, radical and controversial.

> The problem is not so much sycophancy as timidity – his fear of seeming deferential makes for irreverences that are just a bit too hairy-handed: thus he will invariably attempt to balance a slice of royalist homage with some chortling stuff about shitting or masturbation.

This lip-smacking readiness to savage a dear friend and colleague may have had something to do with the fact that TV was making Clive a rich man. He was coining it, and that's not always popular in literary circles. Ian Hamilton would probably have claimed that his ferocity was a sign of his unshakable critical integrity, his insistence on telling it like it is, without fear or favour. But there's a bit too much relish on display here for that to be wholly convincing. Perhaps it's true that there's only so much fame and admiration to go round in any one generation. Perhaps literature's high-minded practitioners really do feel that one writer's rise can only come at the expense of another's fall. Perhaps 'The Book of My Enemy Has Been Remaindered' is not quite as exaggerated as we might have assumed.

The Book of My Enemy Has Been Remaindered

> The book of my enemy has been remaindered
> And I am pleased.
> In vast quantities it has been remaindered,
> Like a van-load of counterfeit that has been seized

And sits in piles in a police warehouse,
My enemy's much-praised effort sits in piles
In the kind of bookshop where remaindering occurs.
Great, square stacks of rejected books and, between them, aisles
One passes down reflecting on life's vanities,
Pausing to remember all those thoughtful reviews
Lavished to no avail upon one's enemy's book –
For behold, here is that book
Among these ranks and banks of duds,
These ponderous and seemingly irreducible cairns
Of complete stiffs.

The book of my enemy has been remaindered
And I rejoice.
It has gone with bowed head like a defeated legion
Beneath the yoke.
What avail him now his awards and prizes,
The praise expended upon his meticulous technique,
His individual new voice?
Knocked into the middle of next week.
His brainchild now consorts with the bad buys,
The sinkers, clinkers, dogs and dregs,
The Edsels of the world of movable type,
The bummers that no amount of hype could shift,
The unbudgeable turkeys.

Yea, his slim volume with its understated wrapper
Bathes in the glare of the brightly jacketed *Hitler's War Machine*.

His unmistakably individual new voice
Shares the same scrapyard with a forlorn skyscraper
Of *The Kung-Fu Cookbook*.
His honesty, proclaimed by himself and believed in by others,
His renowned abhorrence of all posturing and pretence,
Is there with *Pertwee's Promenades and Pierrots* –
One Hundred Years of Seaside Entertainment.
And (oh, this above all) his sensibility,
His sensibility and its hair-like filaments,
His delicate, quivering sensibility is now as one
With *Barbara Windsor's Book of Boobs*,
A volume graced by the descriptive rubric
'My boobs will give everyone hours of fun.'

Soon now a book of mine could be remaindered also,
Though not to the monumental extent
In which the chastisement of remaindering has been meted out
To the book of my enemy,
Since in the case of my own book it will be due
To a miscalculated print run, a marketing error –
Nothing to do with merit.
But just supposing that such an event should hold
Some slight element of sadness, it will be offset
By the memory of this sweet moment.
Chill the champagne and polish the crystal goblets!
The book of my enemy has been remaindered
And I am glad.

3

Japanese Maple

When Clive published his fifth slim volume of thirty-nine short poems in 2015, he, like everyone else, was sure it would be his last. *Sentenced to Life* was focused on the subject of death and dying, with the fierce clarity, intensity and directness that only a man knocking on heaven's door could hope to muster. He had been ill with a clutch of potentially fatal conditions – leukaemia, emphysema, kidney failure and salvo after salvo of recurring carcinomas – since 2010. ('I had the lot,' he says. 'I thought I'd be dropping off the twig any day.') But a happy combination of rapidly advancing medical technology, superb nursing at Cambridge's Addenbrooke's Hospital and sheer luck had kept him going far longer than he or anyone else could possibly have expected.

With the urgency and purpose of a man explicitly living on borrowed time, he had poured all his remaining energies into a feverishly creative spasm of work. He wrote as if his life depended on it, pinging out books about literature, poetry and TV box sets, plugging on with his translation of Dante and completing a highly eccentric verse commentary on Proust, as well as articles and columns for the *Guardian* and other journals. He had also written the *Sentenced to Life* poems, at home and in hospital, by day and by night, driven on by the extraordinary internal flywheel that has made him the most versatile and overproductive writer of his generation.

At the time the first of these poems saw the light of day, a few months before their publication in book form, no-one could possibly have imagined that this little volume was destined to be followed by another poetic farewell, *Injury Time*, which contained more poems (forty-eight) than its predecessor and came out in May 2017. The poignancy of Clive's situation must have coloured people's responses to poems like 'Sentenced to Life' and 'Japanese Maple', but sentiment alone could hardly account for their impact and their immediate popularity on both sides of the Atlantic and around the world.

'Sentenced to Life' was unveiled first, read aloud by Clive on BBC Radio 4's *Today* at breakfast time on 26 May 2014. It didn't stop the traffic, but it stood out a mile in a news and current affairs show that rarely features poetry readings and it triggered a huge response, both in terms of calls to the BBC and enthusiastic social media comments.

The following day, the same programme ran a long, twelve-minute interview by James Naughtie, recorded at Clive's house in Cambridge. Though he was obviously weak, Clive was on fine form, discussing his life and his poems with his usual good-humoured clear-sightedness. He was happy, he said, grateful for the fact that he had his family around him and for the unexpected bonus that he was largely free of pain and still able to work at his writing.

'Even with my health, things could have been worse,' he told Naughtie. 'It could have hurt, for example, and it doesn't. So I haven't got all that much to be miserable about.

'I like to think I have a sunny nature, but a sunny nature doesn't last long if you're in real pain. I've just been lucky.'

The poem's subject matter – disease, guilt, his newly heightened perception of things around him and his memories of Sydney and its Pacific sunsets – was necessarily serious. But despite his 'lungs of dust' and his regrets about personal betrayals, he had written 'Sentenced to Life' with an awareness that maudlin sentimentality was something he should be careful to avoid.

'It's important not to be morbid,' he told Naughtie. 'The secret is to keep a sense of proportion. I'm usually at the hospital two or three times a week. And if you hang around a hospital long enough, you'll see things that'll remind you that you've had a lucky life.'

For those who had known Clive only as a TV host, critic and author and had not been aware of his fifty-year dedication to poetry, 'Sentenced to Life' was bound to come as a surprise. The eight neatly formed, tightly rhymed stanzas contain so many ideas, so many unexpected images, such potent, unflashy turns of phrase. The six goldfish, 'each a little finger long', that glint and swerve in the water of his daughter's pond, 'never touching, never going wrong: / Trajectories as perfect as plainsong', are not new. Before illness sharpened his senses, they would have gone unnoticed. 'But now I catch the tone / Of leaves. No birds can touch down in the trees / Without my seeing them. I count the bees', he says.

The whole poem is an embodiment of Clive's beliefs about how poetry should speak to the reader. It's accessible, even deceptively simple. It's unobtrusively disciplined, shaped but not cramped by the pentameter line and the ABABB rhyme scheme, and it packs a lot in.

'Abundance in a small space' is the phrase Clive uses to define the essence of poetry. 'Value for money. You've got to give them a lot. You've got to give them a bit more than they expect.'

If the reaction to 'Sentenced to Life' was unexpectedly positive, it was nothing compared with the excitement generated when 'Japanese Maple' was unleashed a few months later. The poem was published on both sides of the Atlantic, first in *The New Yorker* and then, the following day, in the *Guardian*, and it was an overnight sensation.

For the first time, Clive had come up with a poem that not only pleased the readers of these publications but was picked up and passed around, on a huge scale, on all the major social media platforms. 'Japanese Maple' went viral, cutting across boundaries of geography, generation and culture. The *New Yorker* website was open, with no paywall to put people off, and the poem quickly notched up a phenomenal 200 000 hits.

'We've had covers or cartoons and occasionally a piece of prose go viral,' says David Remnick, editor of *The New Yorker*. 'Suddenly something is all over the place and bursts out beyond our normal readership. But in 2014, we had an incredibly odd and surprising and wonderful thing happen, when it occurred with this poem called "Japanese Maple".'

No-one had predicted it. The magazine had printed Clive's poems before, without any sensational reaction. This time, though, everything clicked. It was the right poem – right form, right length, right ideas, right imagery – at the right time. Richard Dawkins retweeted it. Jack Seale, a modestly popular British journalist with about 8000 Twitter followers, saw his enthusiastic tweet ('Good lord. Fairly devastating poem by the severely ailing Clive James in *The New Yorker*') retweeted 1300 times in a matter of hours. Suddenly, instantly, 'Japanese Maple' was up there with Robert Frost's 'Stopping by Woods on a Snowy Evening', Dylan Thomas's 'Do Not Go Gentle into That Good Night' and Larkin's 'This Be the Verse' as one of the handful of modern poems that people who don't like modern poetry knew and liked.

Clive has always stressed that it's the writing, not the writer – and certainly not the writer's public status as a poet – that matters. In his 'Letter to a Young Poet', printed as an epilogue to *Injury Time*, he spells it out.

'What matters most is the poem, not the poet,' he says. 'If even a few people remember a line or two in a poem you wrote, you're not just getting there; you're there. That's it: and all the greater glory is mere vanity.'

So when 'Japanese Maple' exploded onto the scene, nobody cared a flying fish whether the author was the beaming TV host who had frolicked in the hot tub with a bunch of beauties at Hugh Hefner's Playboy Mansion or the deeply serious and learned essayist who had written *Cultural Amnesia*, an 850-page survey of the role of the arts in the development and sustenance of liberal democracy – or, indeed, as was the case, both. People just liked the poem, and wanted to share it with their friends.

Why did it speak so immediately and directly to so many people? As with any successful poem, the traditional academic analysis of form and structure, imagery and verbal technique yields no useful answers. Each of the five stanzas is made up of five lines, basically a pair of iambic pentameters (though sometimes much modified, as in the first line), a short line of just four syllables and a rhymed pentameter couplet to finish. The rhyme scheme is ABABB, the same as 'Sentenced to Life'. Masculine rhymes are used throughout, and all the rhymed words except two ('remain' and 'descends') are simple, blunt monosyllables. The poem begins, unusually, in the second person ('Your death') and shifts, halfway through, into the more conventional first person ('Beyond my time, but now I take my share'). All this is true, yet this kind of plodding autopsy tells us nothing at all about how and why the poem works. Even the observation that the rhythms within the metre are handled flexibly, reflecting natural speech patterns, does little to enlighten us.

It is clear that there is a shape, a format or framework that imposes some overall discipline. But the movement of the words plays across that framework in many different ways. The breaks and pauses, the accelerations, slowing-downs and syllabic syncopations are subtle, varied and unpredictable. If you compare the opening line – 'Your death, near now, is of an easy sort' – with the first line of the last verse – 'Filling the double doors to bathe my eyes' – it is clear that the rhythmic effects could not be more different. But, yet again, recognising this takes you no closer to understanding the poem's virtues.

The problem is always there, and always has been. Analysis is not explanation. Pope nailed it neatly, nearly three hundred years ago, in his *Essay on Man*, when he wrote: 'Like following life through creatures you dissect / You lose it in the moment you detect'. Take the poem to pieces and you are left with… a lot of pieces, but no poem.

The central image of the poem is, of course, the little maple tree, *Acer palmatum*, in Clive's Cambridge garden, given to him by his daughter. Its simple, natural beauty is contrasted with the manmade splendour of the Amber Room (originally created in early eighteenth-century Berlin, given as a present to Tsar Peter the Great, looted by Nazi soldiers during World War II and now replicated in the Catherine Palace, near St Petersburg). The tree, a symbol of both life and beauty, becomes the measure by which the dying Clive defines his future. With little hope of seeing out another winter, he sets his sights on surviving long enough to see the maple burn in its autumn glory as the green chlorophyll in the leaves breaks down and the other pigments – reddish anthocyanins and orange carotenoids – become dominant.

> Come autumn and its leaves will turn to flame.
> What I must do
> Is live to see that. That will end the game
> For me, though life continues all the same

The dominant tone of the poem is calm, reflective, appreciative. Autumn, and death, are coming, but their approach is preordained and undramatic. There are no fanfares and no fireworks, just the recognition of 'so much sweet beauty as when fine rain falls' and the glistening that 'illuminates the air' as dusk closes in. The mood is so firmly established that it is quite possible to read the whole poem without noticing the abrupt change of gear that occurs in the last stanza. Suddenly, the autumnal shades that have been viewed from a distance are brought into intimate close-up, 'filling the double doors' and coming closer still to 'bathe my eyes'. The colours become a flood and the intensity mounts until the mind finally switches off, 'burned' by the vision that shines 'so brightly at the last', and fades to black.

I believe it is this final contrast, the dazzling vision followed by the nothingness of death, that gives the poem much of its power. For those of us who steadfastly refuse the promises of religion and see no continuity at all beyond the moment of death, it rings true in a way that few descriptions of the end of life can manage. Clive has often been asked, in the last few years, if his four-square atheism remains unshaken. It does. Tempting as it might be to hope or imagine that something of the person lives on, this is death faced unflinchingly, honestly and with an absolute certainty that exit means exit.

The development of the ideas that run through the poem is gradual. In the first stanza, there is no mention of the maple. The poet is musing on death's slow, inexorable approach, but finding no imagery or parallel for it in the outside world. In the second verse, it is as if he looks aside from his desk and his eye is caught by his rain-soaked Cambridge garden and 'that small tree', newly installed against the left-hand wall. Still, though, it is the rain and the glistening dusk that hold his attention. It is only in the fourth stanza that the focus shifts to the Japanese maple, unremarkable in its early season green foliage, but holding the promise of a blaze of autumnal glory, if only he can live to see it. Though the image of the flaming autumn leaves is the visual centre point of the poem, there are only two lines that talk in any detail about the tree ('My daughter's choice, the maple tree is new. / Come autumn and its leaves will turn to flame'). And even then, of course, it is an image of an imagined future, rather than what is there to be seen.

So why should this particular poem have made such a powerful and immediate impact? Some of the reasons are so banal they hardly need to be spelled out. It is short, which helps. It is built around one striking visual image, familiar to all, much favoured by Japanese poets, but previously unexploited in Western verse. The voice is conversational, personal and not self-consciously 'poetic', slotting easily into a rhyme scheme that seems to shape the poem without imposing any strain. The discipline of form does not lead to forced rhymes or unnatural syntactical inversions and the rhythmic music of the lines lends itself to performance, or, less grandly, to being spoken – or subvocalised – by the reader.

Recent research has shown that subvocalisation, or silent speech while reading, plays an important role in both comprehension and the encoding of memories, so a poem that encourages you to move the mouth and larynx to form the sounds of the words as you read is always more likely to be 'learned' quickly and stick in the memory than one that doesn't. This is a key factor in our subconscious response to poetry, affecting the speed with which we develop a feeling of familiarity with a new poem, and it works to Clive's advantage here.

'Japanese Maple' is not packed with individual lines that call attention to themselves. There is nothing to match the inventively punning power of a Clive James creation like 'Screwed, the planet / Swerves towards its distant, death-dark pocket' (from 'The North Window', his early and affectionate parody of Philip Larkin). But the most haunting lines – 'Your death, near now, is of an easy sort' and 'Burned by my vision of a world that shone / So brightly at the last, and then was gone' – appear at the beginning and end of the poem, in the two positions where they are most likely to be remembered.

This placing is significant. A sensational opening line, like, 'They fuck you up, your mum and dad' or 'Do not go gentle into that good night' or 'Shall I compare thee to a summer's day?', is always a huge advantage, of course, and may well supply a memorable title. But it is often a poem's finale that secures its place in the reader's mind. The poems that end, 'And don't have any kids yourself', 'Rage, rage against the dying of the light' and 'So long lives this, and this gives life to thee' are all perfectly topped and tailed. By contrast, Frost's 'Stopping by Woods', for example, has a curiously tentative, almost querulous, first line, giving little hint of how enchanted we will be by the time we reach the unforgettable ending: 'But I have promises to keep, / And miles to go before I sleep, / And miles to go before I sleep'.

In the case of 'Japanese Maple', both the opening and the final couplet bring together sound, sense and emotion in perfect and well-matched harmony. There are some poems in *Sentenced to Life* and *Injury Time* that could be seen as straying uncomfortably close to sentimentality. In 'Spring Snow Dancer', for example, Clive watches his granddaughter Maia's swift ballet steps as she glides across the kitchen floor: 'And this time I was breathless at the chance / By which I'd lived to see our dear lamb dance – / though soon I will not see her any more.' The scene that's evoked is charming, but the lines seem padded out and contrived (Why 'this time'? Why the ungainly 'at the chance / By which I'd lived to see'? Why 'our dear lamb'?). Maybe it is the fact of reading this poem in the context of a book that deals almost entirely with aspects of death, but the final line ('Though soon I will not see her any more') seems almost redundant, and certainly not one of Clive's best.

By contrast, 'Japanese Maple' is rich, poised and authentic, building steadily towards an ending that seems both moving and inevitable.

Death will come, and it will be final, extinguishing the colours that have unexpectedly lit up the poet's last months and spurred him on to fight his broken body's decline. But death is not what the poem is about. Its subject is life – and the way a heightened sensory and imaginative engagement with it fuels the will to survive. Like the athlete who prepares for a race by visualising and rehearsing the feel of the movements involved, the noise of the crowd and the joy of breasting the winning tape, Clive is setting himself a precise and clearly defined goal, that of surviving until the autumn. There is an implicit contract here, a Faustian bargain. 'Just let me go on that long and I'll be ready,' he proposes. But, of course, when it comes to it, he is going to want more. Another winter, perhaps, another spring, another autumn glory.

This is unmistakably heartfelt, confessional, autobiographical poetry. In a more orderly universe, it should probably have been the last poem to come from his pen. But life, of course, doesn't always keep to the script. As Clive's unexpected survival continued year after year, he became used to the idea that his failure to stick to the predicted timetable was seen as a black mark against him in some circles.

'A lot of people have been quite impatient for my immortality to begin,' he admitted. 'My insistence on hanging around has been seen as a character defect, a bit of a let-down.'

The maple tree, he told one interviewer, was beginning to enjoy its place in the limelight too much. Since the poem had carried its fame around the world, it was showing signs of getting too big for its roots.

'I tell you, that tree, since it's got famous, its whole personality has changed. It gets insulted if you don't pay it attention.'

And there was a certain irony in the air in mid-2016, when he was forced to admit that the original Japanese maple had, embarrassingly, turned its toes up and beaten him to it. It was quickly replaced by a body double, which took over the job of marking the seasons and ticking off the passing of the years, while, inside the house, Clive sat at his desk, glancing out at it for inspiration. Coughing, short of breath and hard of hearing, the familiar domed pate pitted with the scars where aggressive skin cancers had been removed, wearing loose black socks to accommodate his swollen feet, he carried on writing for dear life. *Injury Time* was published in 2017, adding another four dozen poems to the canon, and by the end of the year he had completed the full draft of his longest poem for many years, *The River in the Sky*. He welcomed 2018 with a new poem, 'Season to Season', which made its debut in *The New Yorker* in mid-January, and still the ideas kept on coming, waking him up in the middle of the night and insisting on being written there and then.

'The new poems have to do that,' he told me, 'or they won't get written at all. There's too much going on during the day – admin stuff, hospital visits, writing the last volume of *Unreliable Memoirs*. There's never enough time.'

If 'Japanese Maple' has missed its chance to stand as Clive's lyrical swansong, it is still his best known and most fully realised poem. Whatever else may still be to come from his unflagging pen, it has helped win over the doubters and secure his place as a serious, relevant, accessible and genuinely popular poet. Writing about 'Japanese Maple' in the *Guardian*, the Hungarian-born poet George Szirtes drew a parallel with Robert Louis Stevenson's little eight-line 'Requiem', the source of both Larkin's title 'This Be the Verse' and the familiar ending 'Home is the sailor, home from sea, / And the hunter home from the hill'. Stevenson died and was buried in Samoa, more than 9000 miles from home, in 1894. But he wrote his own epitaph years earlier, in 1880, when he was badly ill in San Francisco. It acquired the extra 'the' ('home from *the* sea') as a result of a monumental mason's error, or a mason's monumental error. Clive, too, is fated to die in exile, thousands of miles from his homeland. But, like Stevenson, he has already written a fine valedictory poem that will live on long after he has gone.

Japanese Maple

> Your death, near now, is of an easy sort.
> So slow a fading out brings no real pain.
> Breath growing short

Is just uncomfortable. You feel the drain
Of energy, but thought and sight remain:

Enhanced, in fact. When did you ever see
So much sweet beauty as when fine rain falls
On that small tree
And saturates your brick back garden walls,
So many Amber Rooms and mirror halls?

Ever more lavish as the dusk descends
This glistening illuminates the air.
It never ends.
Whenever the rain comes it will be there,
Beyond my time, but now I take my share.

My daughter's choice, the maple tree is new.
Come autumn and its leaves will turn to flame.
What I must do
Is live to see that. That will end the game
For me, though life continues all the same:

Filling the double doors to bathe my eyes,
A final flood of colours will live on
As my mind dies,
Burned by my vision of a world that shone
So brightly at the last, and then was gone.

4

In the Heroic Mould

The British public had its first clear glimpse of Clive James as a poet in 1974, when his long mock-epic poem, *Peregrine Prykke's Pilgrimage through the London Literary World*, was performed with a cast of several at London's Institute of Contemporary Arts. Clive took the role of the narrator and Martin Amis played Prykke. The other twenty-something speaking parts were all played by Russell Davies, who presented barely fictionalised versions of everybody from Robert Lowell and Seamus Heaney to the publisher George Weidenfeld and the arts patron Lindy Guinness, the Marchioness of Dufferin and Ava. (I once found myself in the real Marchioness's Holland Park house, described by Wikipedia as 'a popular gathering place for London's "aristo-bohemian set"'. I remember it particularly because of the small but startlingly familiar William Blake original on the landing wall.)

Clive's 2000-line saga, written in rhyming couplets, tells the story of a literary *ingénu* arriving in the capital's vigorously incestuous community of writers and poets, critics and publishers, broadcasters and hangers-on.

Prykke (supposedly pronounced 'Prike', as the first two lines – 'Because so many ask what he was like, / I sing the life and death of

Master Prykke' – would imply, but clearly an early example of Clive's delight in having it both ways) finds himself in an onanistic world of backscratching, log-rolling and mutual congratulation. The big beasts of literary London take him to their hearts, their pubs and their parties, and he is soon ingratiating himself with influential editors with silly names like Ian Hammerhead and Klaus Mauler (not to be confused with *The Listener*'s Karl Miller), who give him a foothold in the London scene and start commissioning reviews and essays from his ever-willing pen.

The hero's rise to prominence closely mirrors that of his progenitor, though, unlike Clive's career, it comes to an abrupt and sticky end, when, in a fit of hubris, he comes to believe himself important and established enough to bite the hands that feed him. Prykke's debut book, *Loose Laurels*, has the gall to suggest that some of the literary gods he has befriended and reviewed so uncritically may be human after all, 'Suggesting So-and-So, though near perfection, / Had minor faults requiring some correction'. In particular, he offers a mortal insult to the American poet identified as Bob Lull: 'Intrepid *Prykke* said *Lull*, by just a skerrick, / Fell short of being totally *Homeric*!' On his way up, Prykke has benefited from the cosy, inbred nature of what FR Leavis scorned as 'the London literary conspiracy'. Now it works against him, as the people criticised in the book are, inevitably, the ones invited to review it.

The result is a catastrophe, as Prykke's career crashes and burns like the Hindenburg zeppelin, a parallel Clive makes vividly explicit.

It was the Book, the Book it was to blame:
The Book that should have reinforced his fame

But punctured it instead and brought it crashing –
Pink flames of hydrogen profusely splashing –
With incandescent girders to Disaster.

Furious at his ingratitude, the big beasts turn and vent their spleen on him. 'Somewhere between polecat and pariah', he is sent to Coventry, damned in print and in person and ejected from the charmed circle.

A crawling bum they'd picked out from the gutter!
They'd known him when his mouth would not melt butter,
And here he was, the two-faced little sod,
Excreting on their stuff like he was God!

Leaving aside the theological insinuations about God's uncouth habits, this is clearly the end of the line for Prykke. There is no way back, and he takes the only course open to him, hitching his belt over a beam and around his neck, balancing for a moment on a stack of Larousse encyclopaedias and Livres de Poche and kicking off to send himself to an early grave.

Despite the sombre ending, *Peregrine Prykke* is predominantly jaunty – upbeat, facetious, frisky and teasing. As a performance piece, it ran for just over an hour, and the ICA audience – largely made up of the very people satirised, and sometimes cruelly parodied, in the poem – obviously enjoyed the experience. Those who were mentioned were flattered; those who weren't felt unfairly excluded. As an exercise in early career self-promotion, *Peregrine Prykke* was a master stroke. But it stemmed from a genuine interest in the heroic epic as a form.

'I love the whole idea of Augustan satire,' Clive told the BBC, forty years later. 'And I thought it should be revived, that we should have another crack at it, because the ideal material was walking around in the form of the literary world. My contemporaries were natural cannon fodder for this kind of poetry. I was rather clumsy at it, I'm bound to admit, but I wrote *Peregrine Prykke's Pilgrimage through the London Literary World* and it became a kind of hit. They all wanted to be in it, even if they were slagged off.'

In his shorter lyric poetry, Clive has always paid close attention to form. Though he has also written free verse, he has experimented over the decades with a wide range of different rhyme schemes, rejoicing in the creative tension between content and the disciplines imposed by form. In *Peregrine Prykke*, however, like so many English poets before him, from Chaucer and Pope to Rupert Bear, he adopts what always seems like the most natural measure for long narrative verse. The rhyming couplet – comfortingly familiar, easy on the reader, relatively malleable and full of opportunities for comic effect – is the default setting.

Like Chaucer and Pope – but unlike Rupert, who, with Swift and Marlowe, favoured the shorter tetrameter line – Clive plumps for the rhymed iambic pentameter. This gives him plenty of scope for ingenuity and variation, including, for example, switching between sharply end-stopped lines and playfully extravagant enjambement (as in the poem's first reference to the *Times Literary Supplement*'s Ian Hamilton, thinly disguised as Ian Hammerhead, 'The famous editor they called the *0 / 07 Bond* of literary *Soho*! / The *TLS*'s frozen-eyed Enforcer / Who thought that poetry went wrong with *Chaucer*!').

The couplet form also has a built-in dynamism, a simple, direct forward thrust that's always likely to be useful in helping propel the reader through a 2000-line epic. But that cuts both ways. It can become a bland, routine drumbeat, and there's an inherent problem when it comes to serving up the necessary 1000 rhyme-pairs.

'On the whole, the couplet suffers the drawback Johnson spotted in the work of Pope,' wrote Clive many years later, in the introduction to his majestic translation of Dante's *Divine Comedy*. 'In a rhyme-starved language like English, the same rhyme sound keeps cropping up too early. Even if the words that rhyme are kept deliberately different each time – night/bright, light/sight etc – the sound is the same, and calls the wrong kind of attention to itself.'

At this stage of his career, Clive had already composed dozens of shorter poems, not to mention a catalogue of more than a hundred songs, written with his musical partner, Pete Atkin, and immortalised in a series of cult-favourite LPs that began with 1970's *Beware of the Beautiful Stranger*. He had tried out a vast variety of forms and rhyme schemes and he knew a lot about the practical pros and cons of the format he chose for *Peregrine Prykke*. In a live performance, where every line and every joke has to hit home immediately or be lost for ever, the predictability of the form has its own advantages. On the page, however, it tends to drag. The rhyming couplets, galloping along, that would have worked just fine in a brief song, spread over fifty pages take their toll. The detail's sharp, satirical and droll, but sometimes even Clive's inventive flair can't quite disguise the formulaic. There are passages of wit, it must be said, but doggerel soon rears its ugly head.

Nobody's perfect. Even Alexander Pope – the master craftsman of the heroic couplet and probably the most quoted English poet after Shakespeare – occasionally struggled to find a rhyme. The man who gave us 'To err is human, to forgive divine', 'A little learning is a dangerous thing' and 'Fools rush in where angels fear to tread' (all in one poem, *An Essay on Criticism*, written when he was just twenty-one) could still get it badly wrong at times. If he hadn't presented us with so many glorious moments, we might easily dismiss him for the banality, weak rhymes and metrical horrors of his worst efforts, such as this misbegotten couplet from the poem 'Windsor Forest'.

Not *Neptune's* self from all her streams receives
A wealthier tribute than to thine he gives.

Clive's 1000-couplet epic certainly contains its own moments of bathos, including plenty of instances where the urgent impulse to deliver a good joke outweighs any other considerations. But there are also many unexpected delights, including, for example, one passage of extreme and explicit eroticism that may be unparalleled in mainstream English poetry. The naïve but newly fashionable Prykke has fallen for the exotic charms of the fragrant, Maserati-driving model and poet Anna Pest (already described, brilliantly, as 'a sight to stop a centaur in mid-gallop'), who whisks him off to her Park Lane pad for a night of sensual pleasure and initiation. As he becomes intoxicated by the heady atmosphere of incense, essences and ointments, the leather and the furs, Perry puts aside thoughts of his loyal girlfriend, Cynthia, and abandons himself to the luxury of his fate.

Adrift in rich pavilions and pagodas
He breathed unnerving, fluctuating odours:
Astringent tangs compounded of *Chanel*
And oysters lying helpless in their shell
He touched an orb of amber rubbed with silk,
He tasted avocados pulped in milk.
She taught him things that felt as nice as flying
And even nicer things that felt like dying.

This is strong stuff, especially in a poem written primarily for public performance. You can imagine some in the audience thinking, 'What was that I just heard?' But, of course, unless they then go on to buy and read *Prykke's Pilgrimage*, they will never hear it again and never be quite sure of anything other than a general impression of intimate and exquisite sexual activity. The moment passes and the story moves on. As Clive knew from his experience of writing song lyrics, there is a huge difference between hearing something once and being able to go back and pore over a written text.

For all its ups and downs, *Peregrine Prykke's Pilgrimage through the London Literary World* went a long way towards putting Clive on the map and signalling his determination to carve himself a career in the metropolitan cultural elite. But there is real poetry here, too. Embedded in the narrative are superb, and very funny, parodies of many of Clive's victims. The bumbling Betjeman, hawkish Hughes and gruffly incomprehensible Seamus Heaney ('Tight mounds brine-splashed with goat-frost. Futtled, numb, / I slop the dunt melt of the scurfing bog's / Black molars to the shred-hung mandrake') are savagely plausible. And while many of the contemporary references no longer mean much, there are plenty of jokes and images that have stood the test of time.

The young Melvyn Bragg is seen uncritically applauding every trendy offering that comes to hand, 'Bestowing many pluses and few minuses / Through perfect teeth, though less than perfect sinuses'. Richard Boston, drinker and founder of the pioneering eco-magazine *Vole*, goes down with all hands: 'Prykke gazed in speechless fright as *Bierstein* drank, / Rolled over like the *Bismarck*, heaved and sank – / A spout of steaming bubbles and low moans / Revealing where he'd gone to *Davy Jones*'.

Margaret Drabble (in the guise of Mag Scrabble) reveals unusual undulatory skills as a belly-dancer: 'She rippled like the skin of a chameleon / Compelled to crawl across a length of tartan – / The sight would have aroused lust in a *Spartan*'. And Prykke himself, flourishing as his career gathers pace, is described in lines that might almost have come from Pope: 'No longer looking wan and undernourished, / He fattened on that magic food, Renown – / The Dish You Know Will Never Let You Down'.

When the *TLS* blog revisited Prykke's world a few years ago, it described the poem as 'wondrous', called for it to be revived and republished and claimed it was 'as fresh as ever'. That could hardly be true. More than half the members of the literary cast list have passed on and the edgy, topical, provocative satire of 1974 has inevitably become a period piece. Time does that. But there's still a lot to savour.

Peregrine Prykke is a ragbag, a bran tub, full of joys for those who care to seek them out. It was included in *The Book of My Enemy*, in 2003, but left out of 2016's *Collected Poems*, which was already a weighty volume. Now Clive and his editor at Picador, Don Paterson, are both keen to see it reprinted.

'It more or less made my reputation,' says Clive. 'I'm fond of it.'

'It's hilarious,' says Paterson. 'It's still hilarious. We've talked about doing something with all four of those longer poems, and repackaging them as a book of miscellaneous excursions, and that'll definitely happen at some point. I think it's well worth reprinting. But then, I think everything Clive does is worth reprinting, so I'm not really the right person to talk to.'

After *Peregrine Prykke* (subtitled *A Tragic Poem in Rhyming Couplets*), Clive went on to produce three more mock-heroic sagas in a similar vein, each, by common consent, a little less successful than the one before. *Felicity Fark in the Land of the Media* followed in 1975. Like *Prykke*, it generated moments of genuine hilarity and a couple of great standalone lines ('The healthy find it hard to like the sick' could have come straight from Pope's *Essay on Criticism*), but its subject matter necessarily meant that it would age less gracefully. The television personalities and critics who seemed, at the time, to embody the spirit of the age have been shown to enjoy a rather shorter shelf-life than their contemporaries among the literary elite. Most of the big media names of the 1970s – the Russell Hartys, Hughie Greens, Bob Monkhouses, Katie Boyles and Lord Longfords – have largely faded from the memory. *Ars longa*, it turns out, *media brevis*. One-nil to the poets.

Clive's next verse epic, *Britannia Bright's Bewilderment in the Wilderness of Westminster*, has been virtually forgotten, to the point where the few surviving copies, published at £1.95, now sell for £50 or more. It is a lightweight piece, full of in-jokes and namedropping, though arguably less flimsy than either *Felicity Fark* or his final venture into this territory, the disastrous *Charles Charming's Challenges on the Pathway to the Throne*. But it was written in 1976, which meant that, entirely coincidentally, it caught the moment when the Heath/Wilson generation of bungling political nonentities finally began to run out of time. The Tory party's internal struggle, from which Margaret Thatcher emerged as Leader of the Opposition, in 1975, forms one of the major episodes in the poem. Ted Heath ('Ted Tede'), Harold Wilson ('Harold Wiles') and Thatcher ('Margo Hatbox') play starring roles, while James Callaghan ('Jokin' Jim') remains, as he did during his time as prime minister, inscrutable, ineffectual and almost invisible.

Clive wouldn't claim any great political prescience. I don't think he foresaw that Margaret Thatcher would change the political landscape for decades to come. But his ear for people's verbal tics and stylistic tricks has always been second to none. He had already recognised the particular quality of Margaret Thatcher's voice two years before, in the *Observer*, when he had likened it to the sound of 'a cat sliding down a blackboard'. Here, given the space within his own poem to nail the suburban clichés and the patronising tone that were to become so familiar over the next fifteen years, he let rip and concocted a Thatcher speech that is almost indistinguishable from many that were actually delivered during the Iron Lady's time in Downing Street.

Britannia Bright's Bewilderment in the Wilderness of Westminster (excerpt)

Her skin peaches and cream, her hair spun gold,

Cucumber-cool with eyeballs ice-cube cold,

She looked like the epitome of poise –

A schoolgirl twice as grown-up as the boys.

Composed of swoops and condescending trillings,

A voice like silver paper on your fillings

Emerged abruptly from the massed loudspeakers.

'We, all of us,' *Hatbox* began, 'are seekers

Of freedom. I am too. Oh gracious, yes.

And yet we'll never cure our present mess

Unless we stop this notion we've been giving

The idle that the world owes them a living.

The welfare system needs to be re-modelled.

Malingerers are being molly-coddled!'

The huge crowd was already on its feet

And stamping so hard *Britt* bounced in her seat.

'Good gracious me,' cried *Hatbox* through the din,

'The time has come to bring back Discipline.

For Heaven's sake, let's end this aimless drift

And start rewarding those who practise Thrift.

We need to back the workers, not the shirkers…'

5

Poetry's Hendrix

It was Saturday 1 October 1966 when Eric Clapton first saw Jimi Hendrix play the guitar. I was there, purely by chance, standing four or five rows back from the stage in the hall at London's Regent Street Polytechnic. And I felt the earth move.

We didn't see it all that night. Hendrix was only on the stage for a few minutes. We didn't see the savage power of 'Purple Haze' and 'Voodoo Chile' or the sweet, liquid lyricism of 'The Wind Cries Mary' and 'Little Wing'. But we saw enough to know that something new and special was happening, right there, before our eyes. The explosive, flamboyant attack and energy, the effortless fluency, the combination of blues feel and electrifying technique – they were unmistakably different. The noisy, glittering, percussive drive, seemingly hovering on the very edge of chaos, was something no-one had ever heard before.

When this unknown guitarist stepped onto the stage in a brown three-piece suit, complete with buttoned-up waistcoat, carrying a chipped and worn right-handed Stratocaster that he played upside down with his left hand, our welcome was distinctly muted. We'd splashed out 7/6 (37.5p) for our tickets and it was Cream – Clapton,

Jack Bruce and Ginger Baker – who we'd come to see. We wanted 'Sunshine of Your Love' and the man Eric introduced, with the brief comment that he was a friend who had just arrived in town from New York, was an interruption.

But everything changed in less than half a minute as the tall, dark stranger flexed his strikingly long fingers and launched into a well-known blues standard, Howlin' Wolf's 'Killing Floor'. This guy was good, really good. Clapton had learned from the Kings of the electric blues – BB, Albert and Freddie – and from Muddy Waters and Buddy Guy. Hendrix didn't seem to have learned from anyone. The music flowed from his fingers, as fresh and spontaneous as if it had come straight from God. As he turned on the showmanship, playing with the guitar between his legs or behind his head or picking with his teeth, we were struck dumb.

When Clapton came back to the mike, he was visibly shaken. In the dressing room afterwards, he reportedly turned on Chas Chandler, who had flown Hendrix to London from New York and brought him along to the gig. 'You told me he was good,' he grumbled. 'You never told me he was *that* fucking good.'

I mention that night in 1966 because I can, because I was there and because I've never forgotten it. I was an accidental eyewitness to a pivotal moment in the history of rock. But there is something about Clive James that reminds me of Hendrix. For one thing, though the bright amber of an early death has preserved the legendary Jimi for ever at the age of twenty-seven, he and Clive were men of the same generation, born just three years apart. If he'd lived, Hendrix would be in his late seventies now – old enough to qualify for a free TV licence, as well as his bus pass.

Both men were blessed at birth with extraordinary talents, with the ability to perform thrilling feats of musical or verbal virtuosity and make it look ridiculously easy. Both were dedicated to developing their gifts, but neither of them was content to wait for the verdict of history. They wanted audiences – big, enthusiastic, appreciative audiences. Growing up in the heady, boundary-breaking days of the 1960s, they wanted people to hear what they could do, understand it and enjoy it.

After producing mock epics like *Peregrine Prykke's Pilgrimage* and light, topically flavoured poems like 'The Book of My Enemy Has Been Remaindered' and 'Bring Me the Sweat of Gabriela Sabatini', Clive was typecast for several decades as an entertainer, rather than a serious poet. The assumption – then, as now – was that you could not be both.

'I wrote lyric poems that were meant to be as deep and intricate as anybody else's,' he insisted, many years later. 'But I still wanted them to pass that first test in front of an audience. I actually did believe a poem ought to be something that could be recited and performed: something entertaining in the first instance. For all the poets, critics and literary journalists who were wedded to the belief that poetry was a private matter, meant only to be overheard, this attitude was anathema.'

While Clive was popping up regularly on the nation's television screens, even those who read his poetry and his serious essays could not bring themselves to recognise their quality. There was certainly no acknowledgement of the fact that the wit and verbal facility that underpinned his TV career might also be relevant to the production of literary works. But virtuoso technique, by its very nature, can often be applied in unexpected ways.

When Jimi Hendrix stood on stage at Woodstock in 1969 and tore into his feedback-drenched performance of 'The Star-Spangled Banner', using his guitar to create the sounds of air attacks, gunfire, explosions and screams of pain, he turned the playing of the American national anthem into an eloquent anti-Vietnam War protest. Many of the tricks and techniques – heavy distortion, octave doubling, sliding chords, high-speed trills, vibrato, slurs, multi-string bends and extravagant use of the tremolo arm – were the same ones we recognised from tracks like 'Purple Haze' or 'Red House'. But this wasn't a high-impact rock number or a 12-bar blues. This was a complete and complex re-imagining of the anthem, transforming its meaning in a way that had never been seen before. It was 'The Star-Spangled Banner' seen from below, from the viewpoint of the cowering victims of America's military might, and redefined through the use of the unique personal vocabulary Hendrix had developed.

For Clive, too, the techniques evolved in one genre are there to be exploited in many different contexts. He takes great delight in this kind of literary cross-dressing. Whole stanzas of his poems turn out, on close inspection, to be long, intricate sentences, built around the kind of complicated syntax of parenthetical comments and subordinate clauses that we would normally expect only in prose. Whole sentences in his essays and TV criticism are lit up by the use of devices – an unexpected rhyme or a staccato burst of alliteration – that are usually found only in poetry. The urge to reward attention, to pay the reader back at every turn for the effort of staying with his words, is the driving force that shapes Clive's style in everything he writes.

The fireworks go off when this concern for verbal texture is combined with startling juxtapositions and fresh, unpredictable ideas. Clive's gift for the pithy insight packed into the outrageously apt phrase has always made reading his journalism vivid and informative. Way back in 1976, before computerisation, when every pilot flew by the seat of his pants, a throwaway TV review of his spawned the line, 'It is only when they go wrong that machines remind you how powerful they are.' More than four decades later, this insight was hideously underlined when two of Boeing's new 737 MAX 8 airliners crashed, killing 346 people, after the planes' flight control systems overrode the pilots' efforts and sent them plunging to their doom.

Whether writing about serious subjects or simply mocking the inanities of light entertainment, Clive has always had this ability to create the kind of phrases that lodge in the memory for years to come. In 1978, a single TV review included the 'terrible fascination' of watching comedians Little and Large fall flat, 'like watching two men share one parachute', and Perry Como doing 'his usual impersonation of a man who has simultaneously been told to say "Cheese" and shot in the back with a poisoned arrow'. When he defined snooker as 'chess with balls' and characterised Formula 1's passionate and excitable commentator Murray Walker as sounding 'like a man whose trousers are on fire', he added new and graphic dimensions to our enjoyment of televised sport. When he wrote a poem ('To Gore Vidal at Fifty') that referred to middle-aged men as being 'Peter Panic-stricken', he summed up the entire premise of a whole generation of novels by authors like John Updike, Saul Bellow and Philip Roth. And when he turned a pitiless spotlight on the aged romantic novelist, Barbara Cartland, and her grotesque make-up, he created an unsettling visual image that still haunts the memory. 'Twin miracles of mascara,' he wrote, 'her eyes looked like the corpses of two small crows that had crashed into a chalk cliff.'

Words were always his tools. He felt the wild, electric energy within them and he relished their unlimited power and possibilities.

In his excellent book, *That's Me in the Corner*, Andrew Collins remembers the time when he and his writing partner, Stuart Maconie, were working with Clive at his television production company in the late 1990s. 'The boys', as the thirty-four-year-old Collins and the thirty-nine-year-old Maconie were known, were given a rough text to work on that had been hashed out by Clive. The draft script contained one particular sentence, quoted in the book, that made Collins wince.

> It was during World War One that the question arose of why
> Franconia and Estonia had joined Korea and the Crimea to seize
> the sisal silos of Silesia and the hairier areas of even scarier Bavaria.

'Instantly recognisable as a Clive James script,' Collins groans. 'The only problem was that it was instantly recognisable as a Clive James script written in 1987.'

I think that's unduly harsh. Leaving aside the sense – there isn't any, and it surely doesn't matter – this torrent of giddy and ridiculous sound-based wordplay strikes me as being on a par with a Hendrix solo. It shows the same delight in virtuosity, the same exuberant energy and the same take-it-or-leave-it confidence. It could only be Clive. Andrew Collins may have been resistant to its charm, but most of us can find something to enjoy there, in the welter of rhymes, alliteration and assonance. Anyone can tap into these well-established techniques. But few would even try to chain them together in such a gloriously tumultuous comic farrago, starting with all the pompous solemnity of a real history book and spiralling, in a matter of seconds, down a yawning plughole of Lewis Carroll-like absurdity. In this case, the aim was to raise a smile. But when Clive turned his attention to more serious matters, he knew he had a rich arsenal of different techniques and effects at his fingertips, honed over many years and ready to be deployed at will.

There is plenty of this technical virtuosity on show in one of the less well-known poems in *Injury Time*. 'Sweet Disaster' is subtitled 'Ronsard Sings of Hélène'. The theme is a familiar one – a May/December relationship, brought to an abrupt conclusion when the younger woman decides 'This has to end', leaving the older man with his tears, his memories and his poetry. 'I have my life to start,' she says, insisting on a clean break, and he knows she means it. From the very beginning, he has been aware that this cannot be a long-term romance. But it has all been worth it: 'And as for me, although I lost, I won / Your love a while, a great thing to have done.'

In this context, 'lost' can't help reminding us of Tennyson's ''Tis better to have loved and lost / Than never to have loved at all', itself probably inspired by Congreve's line ''Tis better to be left than never to have been loved' in his Restoration comedy, *The Way of the World*. But 'lost' also points forward ('although I lost, I won') and 'I won', itself, operates on two levels. We read it first on its own, as the intransitive verb, the paradoxical opposite of 'I lost', and then, an instant later, after the turn of the line, as part of the longer phrase 'I won / Your love a while'. The technical trick, a neat, understated enjambement, is not Clive's private property – enjambement forms part of every poet's toolkit – but it is used here deftly and to some purpose, to redouble the work that is done by an apparently simple and conversational couplet.

On first reading, the poem seems deceptively straightforward in its use of language. The rhythms are those of ordinary speech and the rhymes are mostly single syllables, with just the occasional two-syllable word ('surprise', 'distress', 'supposed' and 'unjust'). There is nothing obviously or self-consciously poetic going on here. But one of the charms of 'Sweet Disaster' is the amount of clever, unobtrusively intricate craftsmanship that lies below the surface, shaping our reactions to the verse without ever drawing attention to itself.

If you want a parallel here with Jimi Hendrix, the obvious comparison would be with a song like 'Little Wing', where he reins in the flamboyant side of his extravagant technique to produce a majestic, shapely performance of extraordinary subtlety and power. The guitar sings like a bird, melodic and wistful, with a poignant alloy of pain and joy. Yet all the trademark Hendrix tricks and techniques are there, deployed with a discipline and restraint that underlines the man's effortless mastery of his art.

'Little Wing' is one of Clive's favourite Hendrix tracks. Fifty years on, in a TV review for the *Telegraph*, he was still reeling from the impact of this 'wonderful music', this 'divine song of God'. If the sixties term 'psychedelic' ever meant anything more than a ragbag of phasing, wah-wah, incomprehensible stream-of-consciousness lyrics and whooshy sound effects, this is it. 'Close your eyes,' Clive writes, 'and you will see visions.'

In 'Sweet Disaster', there is a constant tension between the charged emotion of the situation and the generally conversational tone. When a phrase does stand out, like 'achingly devoid of you' or 'sighing in the grip of bliss', it is not because of any spectacular choice of vocabulary or obvious verbal trickery. The one example of clearly deliberate wordplay is the reference to a 'clean break that no soft soap can mend', a pardonable flash of self-indulgence that slips easily by without disrupting the sense.

Unless you have been reading a lot more carefully than I was when I first met this poem, though, you are unlikely to have noticed the structural pattern that Clive brings to our attention in the final stanza. 'Throughout this poem I have changed the frame / To bring two rhymes together, then apart, / Thus echoing, with one cry from my heart, / Our dance of love.'

It's true, of course, and it's very neatly done. Each of the seven verses consists of a four-line rhymed quatrain followed by a rhyming couplet, but the rhyme scheme within the quatrain alternates between ABBA and ABAB. The first stanza is ABBACC ('law', 'age', 'page', 'more', 'surprise', 'eyes'), the second ABABCC ('to', 'here', 'you', 'near', 'me', 'see') and so on, so the rhymes are literally brought together and moved apart, verse by verse. It's one of Clive's little *jeux d'esprit*, an elegant technical manoeuvre, but does it actually add anything to the poem? Well, obviously not, until one's attention is drawn to it. And isn't there something a bit unseemly about the poet nudging your elbow so blatantly? Yes, probably. But without that, I have to admit, I would certainly not have noticed what was going on. I needed the nudge, so, in the end, I am grateful for it.

Each time I come back to the poem, days or weeks later, my enjoyment of it is enhanced by this awareness of the way the form is shaped to match the content. It's like the pleasure that comes from solving a hard clue in a cryptic crossword, which depends largely on the warm recognition of the common ground that links the setter and the solver, or the satisfaction we get when we hear Cole Porter capering through 'You're the Top', rhyming 'Colosseum' with 'Louvre Museum' and 'Fred Astaire' with 'camembert'. There is joy to be found in excellence, in nonchalance, in boldness, in virtuosity, in Hendrix's soaring, swooping solos, in Clive's audacious wordplay and, here, in his delicate, stately dance of the rhymes.

Sweet Disaster
(Ronsard Sings of Hélène)

> For you, it's easy to lay down the law
> At your age, just a fraction of my age.
> All you need do is turn another page

And suddenly you see my name no more.
Where have I gone? It's almost a surprise,
But all too soon you will believe your eyes

And think I vanished, as you told me to,
From all the world. The world, though, is still here
For me, and achingly devoid of you –
Worse, there are fantasies that come too near
Resembling you. They bend and speak to me
In your voice, whispering, 'What do you see?'

I see you sighing in the grip of bliss:
That much you heard me say, and now you say
Well, that will do. No more for you today,
Or ever. Not a touch and not a kiss.
I have my life to start. This has to end
With one clean break that no soft soap can mend.

Bravely I take it in and hope you lie,
But know you don't, for you are not the type:
Too true by nature. When you caught my eye
I knew already that our time was ripe
To run its course in just a year or less
And end. And now I live with my distress

And it is worse, far worse, than I supposed
It might be when I first became aware

That I would suffer if you were not there.
I still can't bear to see the chapter closed,
And it is months now and will soon be years
That you are not here to behold my tears.

What was achieved? For you, I hope and trust,
Some guarantee there is a gentle touch
A man can have which proves him not unjust
In this dispute where women risk so much:
And as for me, although I lost, I won
Your love a while, a great thing to have done.

Throughout this poem I have changed the frame
To bring two rhymes together, then apart,
Thus echoing, with one cry from my heart,
Our dance of love. Let this, then, be your fame
When you are gone, if it be my fame too,
To find true glory through my loss of you.

6

Game Over

On the last day of 2009, Clive James's life changed for ever. By the time the strains of 'Auld Lang Syne' were ringing out to welcome in the new decade, he was transformed from the ebullient, non-stop, globetrotting, motormouth, motorbrain Aussie we had known for so many decades into a doomed and depleted invalid.

'I had to go in because of sudden kidney failure,' he says. 'I couldn't pee. I had a prostate problem and my urinary tract packed up on me. They had to operate straight away. I nearly died. And while I was there, I was diagnosed with everything else.

'In addition to emphysema, I also had a brand of leukaemia. I nearly croaked twice that year.'

The diagnosis of B-cell chronic lymphocytic leukaemia was not a death sentence in itself, but the outlook was not good. He might live for months, perhaps even years, but there was no prospect of recovery. Treatment would start immediately, but the news that he had three life-threatening conditions was devastating. The world had changed overnight, echoing Clive's favourite line from WH Auden, 'The earth turns over, our side feels the cold', and bringing him up short against the hard truth of his own impermanence.

Ten years earlier, to the day, Clive had hosted ITV's three-hour millennium spectacular, *A Night of a Thousand Years*. He'd sung and danced his way into light entertainment history with a finale consisting of a gruesomely grandiose choreographed version of the Fred Astaire/Ginger Rogers classic 'Pick Yourself Up' that also starred, for various unlikely reasons, Magnus Magnusson, Christopher Lee and Leslie Phillips, Lionel Blair and Sacha Distel, 'It Girl' Tara Palmer-Tomkinson, Felicity Kendal and Helen Mirren. He had already sold his successful TV production company, Watchmaker, and had decided to make this his swansong, quitting television and turning over a new leaf for the next thousand years. No-one on the outside knew it yet, but 'TV's Clive' was turning back to the written word.

The decade between these life-changing moments saw an outpouring of books, essays, journalism, song lyrics and poetry that fully justified the comment his friend Ian McEwan had made after reading a thoughtful, well-balanced *New Yorker* piece Clive had written a few years earlier about the degree to which the German nation, as a whole, had conspired with Hitler in his persecution of the Jews. '*That* is what you should be doing,' McEwan had said, sternly. Like many of Clive's friends, and enemies, he was convinced that the TV work that had made Britain's least-disliked intellectual a household name was a distraction, a profligate waste of his prodigious talents.

Even at the time, Clive had felt the force of McEwan's censure. It took him a while to decide to make the change of direction, but he knew it had to happen.

'I knew he was right,' he wrote in *The Blaze of Obscurity*, volume five of his *Unreliable Memoirs*. 'The time was coming when I would have to get back to bedrock. I still believed my work in television was giving me a wider scope, but here was a reminder that it would take concentration to go deep, and there was only so much of life left.'

How long that 'only so much' might be is, of course, something nobody can predict. Clive had just passed sixty when he pulled the plug on his television career, but those of us who still feel like overgrown teenagers as we move into our seventh decade find it hard to believe that we may be approaching the end of the line. We still believe, deep down, that we will be the exceptions who live for ever, untouched by time or physical frailty. Personally, I've been lucky. For me, the years from sixty to seventy don't seem to have changed anything. But I lost two of my best-loved and most influential contemporaries, the journalist and media guru Nick Van Zanten and the happy-go-lucky adventurer Will Creavin, in their early sixties, and Clive, like the rest of us, was beginning to find himself attending too many memorial services. As he wrote in one of his most moving poems, 'At the Funeral of Ian Hamilton', 'Another black-tie invitation comes: / And once again, the black tie is the long / Thin one and not the bow'. You can't ignore the heavy hints of your own mortality, however hard you try. And if, like Clive, you feel you still have a lot to do, you just have to get on and do it.

For ten years after turning away from the spotlight, his output was extraordinary, in volume, quality and scope. The poems ranged from an updating of Theocritus in 'The Magic Wheel' and the poignant elegy for Ian Hamilton to the mischievous and much-tweeted 'Windows Is Shutting Down' ('Better perhaps, to simply let it goes. / A sentence have to be screwed pretty bad / Before they gets to where you doesnt knows / The meaning what it must of meant to had'). The prose included the mighty (and weighty) *Cultural Amnesia* and the inside story of his days in the TV limelight, *The Blaze of Obscurity*. There were essays, journalism, songs written with Pete Atkin and sixty brilliantly lucid, argumentative and amusing ten-minute programmes for the Radio 4 series *A Point of View*.

But then the blow fell. The onset of his fatal illnesses seemed, at first, to signal the end of this golden period of literary productivity. Clive retreated back to Cambridge, to a little four-bedroomed end-of-terrace house close to his family and just north of Jesus Green and the River Cam. The house was adapted to Clive's needs, with the long kitchen dining room converted into a kitchen study, lined on both sides with bookshelves, with his desk in the middle, lit from above by a broad skylight, and the double doors to his right opening out onto the small, secluded garden. In between painful and exhausting visits to Addenbrooke's Hospital, Clive would spend most of his days reading and his weekends binge-watching box sets of American TV series (*The Sopranos*, *Mad Men*, *Game of Thrones*, *The West Wing*, *Band of Brothers*, *Breaking Bad*, *The Wire*, whatever) with his younger daughter, Lucinda. And yet, in spite of it all, he still found himself driven by the urge to write. He completed the decade-long marathon of translating Dante's *Divine Comedy* (2013), composed *Gate of Lilacs* (2016), an eccentric verse commentary on Proust, compiled two books of brief, energetic literary essays – *Poetry Notebook* (2014) and *Latest Readings* (2016) – and put the box set binges to good use in *Play All: A Bingewatcher's Notebook* (2016), as well as writing a popular series of articles for the *Guardian* under the title, 'Reports of My Death'. (The reference is to a commonly misquoted remark by Mark Twain: 'Reports of my death are greatly exaggerated.' What Twain actually said, in a letter written in London in 1897, was 'The report of my death was an exaggeration.' As often happens in these cases, though, the misquote is probably the better version.)

All the time, however, these activities were being interrupted by the need – felt as an insistent necessity – to write the short, powerful lyric poems that went into *Sentenced to Life* (2015) and *Injury Time* (2017). Clive has said, many times, that he did not ever sit down with the intention of writing poetry during this period.

'I don't write poems for the sake of it,' he told those who came to interview him. 'I try not to finish anything that isn't coming from a really solid idea.'

A particular idea would force itself upon him, demanding to be released. He would often find himself driven by a pitiless combination of inspiration and insomnia into shuffling downstairs in the early hours of the morning and working on a poem till dawn broke and the thoughts had been captured and resolved.

One of the poems squeezed out in these overnight sessions was 'In Your Own Time'. This begins with a retreat from the brink of death, the film running backwards as the narrator goes 'Back to the gate, back to the lounge, back to / The shuttle bus, the same airport hotel'. His departure has been cancelled again. Not that he will be going anywhere when it does finally leave – 'The flight is going nowhere anyway' – except nonstop to oblivion. In the meantime, the extra day, the 'stolen hours', must not be wasted. Someone in his situation must make the effort 'To use the time, to read, to write, to earn / Your keep', not because there is any need for money, but because these are the things that make him who he is. 'What we are is what we do. / Back, then, to what you do best.'

For Clive that means working with words. He must 'Give a thought / The curve of words that makes a wing of it. / Get one more line to sing the way it ought'. There is no mention of an audience now. Though he has spent much of his career stealing the limelight and milking the applause, he's doing this for himself, because he must, for his own satisfaction, 'as if your fate / Depended on the balance of a phrase'.

Don Paterson, his friend and editor, has seen the way this determination to write everything he wants to write, while he has time, has spurred him on.

'Clive projects himself into the future through his books,' he says. 'These days it keeps him going where folk who'd asked less of themselves would have dropped.'

For anyone who has watched Clive through these last few years, it is obvious that this is literally true. As his strength has ebbed, the little house has become his world, a world he hardly leaves except for hospital visits. Work and family are now the only things that matter. But he is still pushing himself to write, to get it all down, and his delight in the exercise of his skills is evident in every conversation about his current projects. 'In Your Own Time' ends with a frank acknowledgement of the pleasure he still gets from the work: 'The thrill of getting things exactly right / Prepares you for the long flight through the night.' He's not trying to impress anybody any more. The standards he is using to measure the success of each line are entirely his own.

'In Your Own Time' is impeccably formal in its structure. It consists of four six-line stanzas of rhymed iambic pentameters, using the ABABCC 'Venus and Adonis' rhyme scheme (also known as *sesta rima*) that Shakespeare borrowed from Spenser. The carpentry of the lines is careful and meticulous, but the impression is by no means stiff. The rhymes are carried by simple, mainly monosyllabic, rather humdrum words, and the rhythms flow and break with the unforced ease and natural syntax of ordinary speech. The effect is conversational and engaging, as if the poem is shaped by its form without being restricted by it, and the one line that seems self-consciously overworked – 'Anything well-expressed is holy writ' – can probably be forgiven for trying too hard to achieve a provocative double pun.

The other 'Time' poem in the 2017 collection – and the one that gives the book its name – is 'Injury Time'. This is less optimistic; there is no implication here that the plates can be kept spinning for ever as long as the dying man can keep on writing. Death has been deferred, but the final whistle will go at any minute. The tone of Clive's poem is resigned and calm, tempered with a sense of bemused curiosity at the fact of his continued existence.

> This is a pretty trick the fates have played
> On me, to make me think that I might die

Tomorrow, and then grant me extra time.

Each night he goes to bed half-expecting to die in his sleep, slipping into the same modest dream of surviving, 'still not dead', to face the unexpected bonus of another day. While the rest of us toss and turn in nightly sequences of surreal danger and drama, lurid excitement and trouser-less or food-splattered embarrassment, he just dreams of waking up alive. I was once married to someone, placid and easy-going by day, whose recurring nightmare involved running for her life across a ploughed field, pursued by a giant and grimly malevolent potato. Clive dreams only of coming downstairs and resuming his existence, until that final morning when his notebook, lying there untouched, will signal that the end has come. And each morning, so far, the dream has come true. The only certainty is that this won't go on indefinitely, but the end result has been so long anticipated that it has almost been discounted. It will happen, and when it does, that's that.

'Injury Time' is tight, spare and underplayed. The sonnet form uses a strict, if unusual, rhyme scheme and the five-stress iambic pentameter lends a sense of quiet poise and authority. But there is a subtly inventive flexibility within Clive's chosen structure. Most sonnets, for example, have a break – the turn or *volta* – where the poem changes direction. There will usually be a marked change of pace or twist in the argument – often, in the Italian tradition, after eight of the fourteen lines; sometimes, as in Shakespearean or 'English' sonnets, just before the final couplet. In Clive's poem there is a clear turning point, but it falls between the tenth and the eleventh lines, where he shifts from describing his evening routine to looking ahead ('This nightly dream can turn out to be true / Only so long'). These last four lines are also set slightly apart by their rhymes ('true', 'notebook', 'took', 'do') and by the break from the conventional iambic da-DUM, da-DUM metre into a more supple, speech-based rhythm, culminating in the stately conclusion: 'To show how long it took / Silence to do what it was bound to do'.

The striking central image of the poem – the 'Himalayan slog upstairs to bed', which 'might as well be straight into the sky' – brings with it biblical echoes of the ascension, as well as emphasising how laboured and precarious this everyday business of climbing the stairs is for a man in Clive's condition. And the detail of having to place each foot so tentatively, as if treading 'on rolling logs', has its own nightmare quality. We can't easily imagine how someone as weakened and ill as Clive feels inside, but these few lines give us a momentary glimpse of how it must be when all your strength and co-ordination have been drained away.

There is something neat, complete and classical about this sonnet, with its emotional and structural discipline and its elegant, measured execution. There is no sentimentality or polemicising. There are no extravagant lunges into dazzling wordplay, obscure cultural or historical references or grungy street talk – none of the extremes that habitually delight some of Clive's readers and enrage others. It is just a thoroughly well-made poem, taking us, vicariously, into aspects of living and dying that few of us will ever encounter for ourselves.

In the late 1950s, while he was meant to be studying for his first degree at the University of Sydney, Clive devoted a lot of his energy to his role as literary editor of the university's student newspaper, *Honi Soit*. In 2015, shortly before the publication of *Sentenced to Life*, he gave the same paper an unusually frank interview about the poems he was writing and the new perspectives he'd gained from his long battle with terminal ill-health.

'The book is full of things I couldn't have written when I was young and strong,' he told the student interviewer. 'There is no young man's version of what I am writing now.'

Having already been to the brink of death several times and survived to tell the tale, he felt he had been given privileged access to the kind of subject matter that is beyond most people's experience.

'I am in the position of talking with the authority of someone who has been somewhere, like an astronaut who has been to the moon,' he said.

'Apart from bravery, fitness, a science degree and the ability to fly, the main difference between the astronaut and myself is that he got back. I won't be getting back from this. But I am glad to have made the voyage.'

Injury Time

> This is a pretty trick the fates have played
> On me, to make me think that I might die
> Tomorrow, and then grant me extra time.
> By now I feel that I have overstayed

My welcome. Every night I face the climb
Which might as well be straight into the sky:
The Himalayan slog upstairs to bed,
Placing my feet so carefully I seem
To tread on rolling logs, and there I dream
I come back down next morning, still not dead.
This nightly dream can turn out to be true
Only so long, and one day this notebook
Will lie untouched, to show how long it took
Silence to do what it was bound to do.

7

The Locked Ward and the Trouser Thief

The bow-wave of medical advances that has kept the ailing Clive alive, pushing his eventual death further and further into the future, has done us all a great service. Alongside his autobiographical epic, *The River in the Sky*, the two slim volumes that have cemented his stature as a serious poet have given us nearly ninety new poems, all written during his prolonged, expectant wait at death's door.

But the course of this precarious battle for survival has not been smooth. The unending procession of drugs, treatments and operations, crises and recoveries, has taken him to the brink and back so many times that he has become humorously philosophical about it.

'People can't wait for your immortality to start,' he told *the Spectator*'s Sam Leith in August 2017, seven years after he was first warned the end was nigh. 'Your credibility starts to evaporate if you're still around.'

One of the lowest points, though, occurred relatively early on, when his mind, rather than his body, seemed to have let him down.

This uniquely witty, erudite man found himself locked up for ten long weeks as an involuntary patient in the secure psychiatric unit at Addenbrooke's Hospital, after the drugs he had been given –

in particular, the steroids – completely upset his mental equilibrium and triggered a major psychotic reaction.

'I was nuts,' he says, simply. 'I was bouncing off the walls.'

This devastating turn of events took place in 2011. But no-one on the outside knew what was happening to him. There were no announcements, no news stories about his plight, no cruel tabloid headlines shouting 'Clever-clogs Clive locked up in funny farm'. It wasn't until *Injury Time* was published, six years later, with two poems explicitly talking about this shattering experience, that anyone other than Clive's family and a few close friends could know what he'd been through. Even then, the critics and reviewers seemed not to notice what was clearly spelled out in 'Not Forgetting George Russell' and 'Recollected in Tranquillity'.

The George Russell poem is a tribute to a man Clive revered as a great friend and teacher, a scholar who edited the definitive C-text edition of Langland's fourteenth-century masterpiece *Piers Plowman*, but also once ambushed his undergraduate students by running a surprise class on the movie *Trainspotting*. The poem begins with a chillingly frank description of life in the Closed Ward at Addenbrooke's.

How funny, in the sense of not being funny,
It ought to be that here, on the nut farm –
A Cambridge feature Rupert Brooke left out
For obvious reasons –
In a cool morning when all except the nurses
Are tranked out of their skulls,

I haunt the kitchen reading an old essay,
Trying to find my tone again

The second poem that talks about this period is even more detailed and disturbing. The title plays on Wordsworth's assertion in his *Preface to Lyrical Ballads* that poetry is 'the spontaneous overflow of powerful feelings' taking its origin from 'emotion recollected in tranquillity'. But Clive's 'Recollected in Tranquillity' conjures up a nightmare madhouse scene straight out of an old Ken Russell movie, a 'Babelic rumpus room' he shares with a cast that includes 'the Trouser Thief and the lady with one song she sang forever'.

'It was a tough time, the toughest time I've had while I've been sick,' Clive told me. 'We found out the hard way that I've got a low tolerance for steroids. For a long time after it was over I made sure nobody knew about it, as I didn't want all my press coverage to be about whether or not I was mentally well. It was a bad few weeks – and it seemed like forever.'

Unbalanced but still self-aware, he struggled at first to convince the hospital staff that it was all a terrible mistake. As the poem says, 'My brain teemed / With stuff to tell the doctors so they might / Unbolt the door, but that place was a tomb / Sealed tight'. After a while, of course, he realised that insisting he was sane – or, for that matter, Napoleon, Jesus or Buddha – would only appear to confirm the diagnosis. The staff in places like this have heard it all too many times before.

'The thing to do was to sit still, make as little fuss as possible, and wait. For a man who has always acted on impulse, which I'd been doing all my life, that was a new discipline to learn. But I made notes, and I told myself they'd turn into something when I got out of there. You store things away.'

On one level, he was confused, suffering and heavily sedated. On another, he was coldly aware of the way the trauma he was going through might one day be mined for literary gold. The *dramatis personae* – the zombified patients, the woman who sang her one plaintive song night and day and the man who was driven to steal other people's clothes – were so far outside the realms of his previous experience that he knew he would eventually find himself writing about them.

'I felt I could have hugged the Trouser Thief, because I knew he was going to be a future theme. It was as if he'd just been sent from Central Casting. And I thought about George Russell, who was already dead, and figured out a way I'd be able to write about him when I could. What I had to get used to was the idea that I couldn't develop these themes then. They'd have to wait.'

Once the steroid doses had been adjusted to re-establish the right balance, Clive's mental state returned more or less to normal, though the physical challenges caused by his leukaemia and several aggressive bouts of pneumonia took him very close to the exit at least three times in the next eighteen months. It was more than five years before he was ready to mention this aspect of his ordeal in his published poetry. Although *Sentenced to Life* includes so many poems that touch directly on the themes of mortality and morbidity, there is nothing in that collection that talks about the closed unit and the locked doors. When *Injury Time* came out, early in 2017,

Clive half-expected the press coverage to pounce on the revelation that he had spent weeks as an involuntary patient in a psych ward.

'In a way, it was unflattering that nobody noticed,' he told me. 'I suppose you know, deep in your heart, that the people who dash into print with their reviews – even the most positive ones – won't all have read all the poems, even in a slim volume like this. But I was surprised that no-one at all picked up on it. You'd have thought that the press, who have been quick enough to clamber over other aspects of my personal life, would have spotted it and made something of it. After all, madness and poetry have always gone together in the public imagination.'

He was right, of course. There is a long tradition that connects poets and mental illness – from Cowper and Blake, Christopher Smart and John Clare to Ezra Pound, Sylvia Plath and Robert Lowell. And that's before you start thinking about the other important poets whose behaviour was so bizarre and excessive that their contemporaries assumed they were mad, even if the doctors were not sure. Pushkin and Swinburne, Edgar Allan Poe and Emily Dickinson, Baudelaire and Dylan Thomas, and, before them, Thomas Wyatt (who liked to live close to the edge and was said to have had an ill-advised affair with Anne Boleyn) and Lord Rochester were all widely regarded as more than merely eccentric. Poor Byron – brilliant, handsome, gifted, reckless, priapic, deformed, abused, bisexual, incestuous and obsessive, and given to keeping bears, monkeys, herons, badgers and goats around the house – certainly seemed to his contemporaries as near to insane as any man could be. It was just his historic misfortune, despite his status as a truly great poet, that no single line of his has penetrated the English language as thoroughly as the comment by his lover, Lady Caroline Lamb, that he was 'mad, bad and dangerous to know'.

According to one academic study, published, ironically, in 2011, the poet is twenty times more likely to end up in an asylum than the non-poet. But few of these tortured souls have suffered from purely medically-induced problems. Once Clive's oversensitivity to steroids was recognised, he was able to recover the mental powers that have led to a vast and wide-ranging outpouring of poetry and prose in his later years. And he was also able to learn from what he had endured.

Looking back on it all, years later, he felt he had gained new insights from what had happened to him.

'I found out a lot about how the mind controls itself,' he told me. 'You have to go right to the edge, where it isn't controlling itself, to find out. It's like the way Michael Schumacher used to drive. He was always out of control, not in it. Outsiders didn't understand this, but all the Formula 1 drivers did. All the other drivers went up and up, edging closer and closer to the limit where you lose adhesion. Schumacher was different. He was always *over* the limit and always just pulling himself back.'

But there was something that was lost for ever when Clive went through his private hell, the 'sad spell of frenzy' that he felt summed up a whole life that 'had been a greedy fever'. As the poem explains, he and his family knew he was irreversibly changed: 'Something ill-mended in my mind demands / I live alone. And so they come and go / To help me do that'.

The domestic set-up that has underpinned the literary productivity of Clive's last few years has been fine-tuned to meet his needs. His daughter Claerwen is next door, while his wife, Prue, and his other daughter, Lucinda, live a few minutes away, round the corner.

'I live alone. But I live alone only on the understanding that they barge in every five minutes,' he says. 'Having-It-Both-Ways is my middle name.'

The poem that deals most explicitly with his psychotic episode and its aftermath is 'Recollected in Tranquillity'. It is a remarkable poem in many ways, and not just because of its revelatory content. Its form, too, is unique, and quite unlike any of Clive's other poems.

'Recollected in Tranquillity' consists of five rhymed verses, each eleven lines long, except for the third stanza, which has only ten lines. It is, on the whole, tightly and conventionally rhymed, with only one unobtrusive slant rhyme ('lull' and 'downfall') and a handful of lines (just six out of fifty-four) that do not rhyme at all. But the poem's rhyme scheme is extraordinary, as it modulates from verse to verse, so that each of the five stanzas takes a different form. Reading it raises the question – which, I admit, had never occurred to me before – of what rhyme is actually for.

At the most basic level, it is obvious that using rhyme helps to give shape and unity to a poem. It creates audible echoes between the elements of a verse – sometimes loud and forceful, sometimes muted and almost unnoticed.

In this poem, the first stanza is built around a series of fairly blunt and uncomplicated rhymes. 'Delay', 'day' and 'say' link the second, fourth and eighth lines, while the rhyming pairs 'ends' and 'friends', 'years' and 'tears' and 'alive' and 'arrive' bolt together the elements of the verse within the brackets created by the first and last lines ('reprieve' and 'leave').

> You realise that this is no reprieve
> But merely a delay?
> The comedy must end. The way it ends
> Has just been put off for another day.
> Perhaps two months from now, perhaps two years,
> It will be known to family and friends
> That you, at last, are more dead than alive,
> With nothing left to say.
> When any tears there are will be their tears,
> Not yours, the wave of silence will arrive
> With which you leave.

But the fourth stanza, for example, works in a very different way. A series of understated, unemphatic rhymes ('set free', 'for me', 'finally') creates a faint link between the first, fifth and eleventh lines. Lines two and four rhyme, as do lines three and nine, six and eight, and seven and ten. There are no loose threads, no orphaned line-endings, in this stanza. Yet there is no build-up of expectation, because there's no way we can anticipate, as we read, when the next rhyme is due to arrive.

The point is that rhyme usually goes some way towards telling the reader what to expect. If the rhyme scheme is tight and regular, as in rhyming couplets or four-line ABAB stanzas, this predictability can be a disadvantage, especially if it is combined with the kind of metronomically insistent marching rhythms that characterised so much second-rate Victorian poetry. With the metre telling you when to expect the next rhyme and the foreknowledge that the line-ending will chime with a sound you have already heard, a sort of mental triangulation takes place that makes many rhymed lines seem dully inevitable. You read 'June' and you're waiting for 'moon'. You read 'part' and you wait for the obligatory 'heart'. It's an old problem. As Alexander Pope protested so eloquently in 1709,

> Where'er you find 'the cooling western breeze',
> In the next line, it 'whispers through the trees':
> If crystal streams 'with pleasing murmurs creep',
> The reader's threatened, not in vain, with 'sleep'.

At its worst, rhyming verse can become as four-square and unvarying as a staircase: safe, repetitive and unexciting. If it's handled more subtly and inventively, though, rhyme can provide form and variety, light and shade, offering touchpoints, connections, handholds and points of reference that help the reader pick out a route and get to grips with the poem.

'I like that image,' said Clive, when we discussed this. 'We're on our way to a good metaphor there. We're traversing a rock face. The pitons have to be driven into the rock, smacked in to the right depth in just the right places.'

Irregular, fluid and shifting rhyme schemes occur more frequently than we usually realise in English verse, in everything from Matthew Arnold's 'Dover Beach' to Eliot's 'The Love Song of

J Alfred Prufrock' and the poems of Wallace Stevens. In 'Recollected in Tranquillity', the long and unpredictable intervals between the rhymed words mean that we lose all sense of expectation. By the time we get to hear the rhymes – 'reprieve' and 'leave' in the opening verse, with nine lines in between them, and 'free', 'me' and 'finally', scattered across the fourth stanza – the rhyming effect is almost subliminal.

On top of this, the variations and inversions make each new stanza seem almost like a new poem. The first two verses are both complete statements, each of them finished and whole, rounded off with a decisive full stop. The third – the shocking ten-line stanza that describes Clive's dazed and tormented period in the locked ward at Addenbrooke's – is more open-ended. Its final thought ('I ate my sleeping pills and dreamed / Of all I could have had') makes sense as it stands but also rolls over into the first line of the next stanza ('The happiness I wasted') to create a sort of conceptual enjambement. You can read it either way, or both. And the link between the last two verses is clear and explicit. The distinct rhyme schemes separate the two stanzas, but the sense and the syntax work hand in hand to bring them together ('And nightfall finally / Blankets my vision of this bright arcade').

In this last stanza, the emphasis is on Clive's devotion to his literary career, the motivation that has kept him alive and active through his long physical decline. Whenever the end comes, he knows there will still be a 'burial mound' of 'treasured papers' and his black Chinese notebook full of 'unfinished thoughts' on his desk. The rhyme scheme twists yet again, one last time, with no end rhymes in sight in the last couplet, but a neat internal rhyme ('despair') echoing the triple rhyme ('air', 'chair' and 'there') that has run through the stanza, as it builds up to the final punchline: 'I loved it here.'

The whole structure of the poem leads to this focal point. Clive's mind ran amok during this cruel psychotic episode, before regaining its equilibrium and allowing him to become himself again, and he sees the way the poem develops and its unsettled rhyme scheme as reflecting this turbulence.

'This is a strange one,' he told me. 'It's got to turn around on itself. It goes haywire six different ways so that it can come round to there in the end: "I loved it here." That's what I feel, and it's what I wanted to say.'

Recollected in Tranquillity

You realise that this is no reprieve
But merely a delay?
The comedy must end. The way it ends
Has just been put off for another day.
Perhaps two months from now, perhaps two years,
It will be known to family and friends
That you, at last, are more dead than alive,
With nothing left to say.
When any tears there are will be their tears,
Not yours, the wave of silence will arrive
With which you leave.

THE LOCKED WARD AND THE TROUSER THIEF

So this must be the storm before the lull,
These webs of words
Slowly assembled at the summer's peak
Here in the portico of your downfall,
As you sit watchfully to count the birds –
So few beside the Heathrow rush of spring –
Which in the garden briefly peck and preen
Before continuing
To Finland, Iceland, Baffin Land, wherever:
Your chance to speak before you never speak
Again, your next to final scene.

This peace, which will be perfect by and by,
Came out of chaos. When the drugs went wrong
It almost seemed a burden not to die
As I shared that Babelic rumpus room
With the Trouser Thief and the lady with one song
She sang forever. Racing, my brain teemed
With stuff to tell the doctors so they might
Unbolt the door, but that place was a tomb
Sealed tight. I ate my sleeping pills and dreamed
Of all I could have had –

The happiness I wasted. Now, set free,
I see that my whole life
Had been a greedy fever. A sad spell
Of frenzy only summed it up. My wife
And daughters built this studio for me

In which I read and write and rest. They know
Something ill-mended in my mind demands
I live alone. And so they come and go
To help me do that, and so all is well,
As I wait for the day the last bird lands
And nightfall finally

Blankets my vision of this bright arcade.
Outside, in that cane chair,
I sat to read *The Faerie Queen* and found
Garbled accounts of knights and damsels made
Melodic sense, in verse as light as air.
On this desk, crowded as a burial mound
With treasured papers, my Chinese notebook,
Full of unfinished thoughts, will still be there,
When I, at last, can't reach it. Should things look
As if I knew despair, of this be sure:
I loved it here.

8

A Chip of Ice in the Heart

Clive James was cast away for the first time in 1980, when Roy Plomley was still presenting *Desert Island Discs*, and brought back again twenty years later to talk to Sue Lawley. He is one of the elite group of about two hundred and fifty castaways who have made two visits to the island in its seventy-seven-year history. He still lags behind his fellow-Aussie Barry Humphries (three and counting) and he is never going to catch up with the only two titans of broadcasting to have been there four times, comedian Arthur Askey and national treasure Sir David Attenborough. But appearing on the programme even once confers a sort of immortality, especially now that all but the earliest shows can be heard again via the BBC iPlayer.

Listening back to the two radio programmes throws up some interesting contrasts. The forty-year-old Clive who appears alongside Plomley in 1980 spends most of the interview seeming surprisingly earnest and po-faced. His eight records are all performances by female vocalists, with five classical pieces, featuring singers like Maria Callas and Elisabeth Schwarzkopf, one Billie Holiday track, The Supremes' 'Baby Love' and, tucked in at the end, a recording by Julie Covington of a beautiful little song, 'If I Had My Time Again', written in the early 1970s by Clive and his lifelong musical partner, Pete Atkin.

The conversation covers his life and his career as a journalist, critic and TV presenter, more or less in chronological order, without any mention of his poetry until quite near the end. Even then, the only references are to three of his long performance poems, the humorously satirical epics, *Peregrine Prykke's Pilgrimage Through the London Literary World*, *Felicity Fark in the Land of the Media* and *Britannia Bright*, all written in a couple of years in the mid-1970s. There's nothing at all about his shorter poems, and nothing to indicate that he had been writing more serious poetry ever since he started at university in Sydney, more than twenty years before. Plomley's unchallenging interviewing style, once described as 'bowling underarm', means the programme was always destined to be polite, deferential and, by any modern standards, blandly unrevealing.

The Clive James of the second *Desert Island Discs* is very different. Sue Lawley's probing, well-researched questioning digs deeper, nudging and inviting Clive to talk much more frankly. She leads him into revelations about his hopes and fears, his attitudes to women, his compulsive busyness and craving for attention, his voluntary exile from his homeland, his constant dread of being revealed as a talentless phoney and about what they both call (borrowing a phrase from Graham Greene) the 'chip of ice' in his heart. The choice of songs is broader and more obviously personal this time around. There's another Billie Holiday and another Atkin/James composition, an Alison Moyet track, a tango song, Jelly Roll

Morton and Frank Sinatra, just one classical piece (tenor Tito Schipa singing Donizetti) and his all-time favourite ('If you could save just one of these eight records...'), Elvis Presley's 'Jailhouse Rock'. Poetry takes a bow within the first few minutes, with Clive reciting a few lines from an early poem of his about a close friend, an obsessively ambitious motorcycle racer, who died in a high-speed crash at Sydney's Mount Druitt racetrack.

The poem, 'The Young Australian Rider, P.G. Burman', is obviously heartfelt. In its full form, it lacks the compact intensity Clive would probably have wanted, but it does contain one chillingly powerful line. The day after the fatal accident, Clive, who has been away with the army, doing his compulsory national service, hears the news from neighbours and is surprised by his own reaction. 'It's not that I felt nothing. I felt nothingness', the poem says. That sense of the void gaping where we expect to feel a more conventional grief is a potent flash of insight and leads the poem to an unexpected conclusion: 'I had one thought before I turned away / The trouble is, with us, we overreach ourselves'.

'I'm still pleased with that last line,' he tells Lawley, 'but I don't quite believe it. I think probably the good thing about us is that we *do* overreach ourselves. We do try things and I'm very glad he did all that. He just got unlucky. You can see why luck obsesses me.'

The ice chip in the heart, which has come up already, early in the programme, in relation to the way Clive left his widowed mother to fend for herself in Australia while he made his career in England, shows itself again in his readiness to use this tragedy as subject matter for his poem about his friend's death.

'Everything's on the agenda,' he says. 'Any writer has a moment of self-loathing when something terrible happens in the life of someone near him and, at the very moment it's happening, he thinks "I can use this".'

Later in the programme, after a string of interesting titbits about music and life (including Mussolini's son's revelation to Clive that Il Duce was an avid Fats Waller fan), they return to the subject of poetry. They've been talking about the familiar charge that Clive's TV career amounted to selling his intellectual soul for a lucrative mess of pottage and Sue Lawley asks him about an early sonnet entitled 'Neither One Thing Nor the Other', about his Cambridge contemporary Stephen Hawking, which ends with the line 'Why am I not profound?'

'I didn't really mean that,' says Clive. 'Secretly, if you read between the lines, I think I am quite profound. Otherwise, why would I be asking the question? One tries to have it all ways. When I get accused of wanting to have my cake and eat it, my only answer is "What else are you supposed to do with cake?"'

The enduring appeal of *Desert Island Discs* has always been based on its simple, undemanding formula. Within the framework of the castaway's choices – eight records (including one particular favourite), one book and a single luxury item – and a loosely structured conversation, it provides an opportunity for everything from intensely personal reminiscences and confessional revelations to tightly controlled image-building. Sometimes the portrait that listeners are offered is little more than a glossy PR construct. Sometimes it highlights aspects of the guest that would have his or her public relations handlers throwing themselves off the nearest cliff. The format doesn't force the issue, and the interviewers, over the years, have never seen themselves as inquisitors. But if you give some of these egos enough rope, they will find their own ways to hang themselves. Oliver Reed demanded a blow-up sex doll as his luxury item. Simon Cowell asked for a mirror, 'because I'd miss me'. (Lawley: 'You going to let us broadcast that?' Cowell: 'I don't care.') Graham Norton wanted a mirror, too, but claimed it was to save his sanity by confirming that he still existed. Norman Mailer wanted a stick of the finest marijuana. Michael Caine, against the sage advice of a world-weary production team, insisted on naming 'My Way' as his favourite song, adding, artlessly, 'It could be me talking.' Other castaways are touchingly candid about their demons and vulnerabilities. Stephen Fry, for example, chose a suicide pill as his luxury. Clive's own choices were less revealing – a newfangled Space Invaders machine in 1980, and a pianola that played the backing tracks to Caruso's songs, so he could develop his singing, in the later programme.

The picture of Clive that emerges from his second *Desert Island Discs* appearance is that of a man in transition. The show went out in June 2000, just months after ITV had chosen him to usher in the new era as Master of the Revels for the three-hour millennium marathon *A Night of a Thousand Years*. He was one of the best-known faces in the land, but he had already taken the decision to cast off the 'velvet shackles' of his television career, step back from the noise and glitter and dedicate himself to his writing – books, essays, journalism, songs and poetry. Though he had already published five books of essays and literary criticism, three bestselling volumes of his autobiographical *Unreliable Memoirs* and a slim volume, *Other Passports*, of poems he'd written between 1958 and 1985, the television was getting in the way. Despite his legendary appetite for work, it ate up his time and energy. It also affected the way people approached his output. People are used to seeing chat show hosts, stand-up comedy stars, failing politicians and heavy metal drummers develop sudden literary pretensions, and they know just how banal the results can be. The corny, formulaic novel, the celebrity cookbook, the half-baked memoir or the routine potboiler about the timeless genius of Churchill or Shakespeare is bad enough. But poetry? Please.

The big difference, in Clive's case, was that he had always been a practising poet, before, during and after his high-profile television career. There was already ample evidence that he knew what he was doing, had an encyclopaedic knowledge of poetry ancient and modern and had grafted for decades to hone his skills. But it was still hard for him to persuade readers to focus on the work, rather than the man behind it, the genial, quirky, occasionally acid, sometimes ingratiating, incessantly word-juggling entertainer they thought they knew from the box.

'Having been blessed, or cursed, with the knack of earning my bread in show business, I was seldom regarded as a proper professional poet, and for a long while had no poetic reputation to speak of,' he wrote a few years later, 'except perhaps as a kind of court jester who was occasionally allowed to perch in a window niche and sing a lament over the ruins of the night's revelry.'

The portrait presented on *Desert Island Discs* is always, ultimately, controlled by the guest. The castaway can choose what is revealed and what is held back, adding a dab of colour here and there with a touching personal story or blanking out those details that are not for public consumption. But a painted portrait cannot be steered and managed like this. The sitter is in the hands of the artist, exposed to a different and more penetrating scrutiny. And while it may be bracing to see ourselves as others see us, it can be unsettling, too. When Clive sat for his friend Sarah Raphael, the brilliantly talented daughter of Oscar-winning screenwriter and *Glittering Prizes* author Frederic Raphael, he was taken aback by the results. He was impressed by the meticulously detailed image, with its inscrutable, unsmiling face and massive, heavily muscled forearms. But he was also bemused.

'If only I didn't look so very isolated and inward-turned,' he said of it, 'as if self-sufficiency had been bought at the cost of losing contact with the world. That can't be right. But what if it is? What if she knows better than I do?'

The other major portrait of Clive, by Jeffrey Smart, 'the Australian Edward Hopper', shows him as a tiny figure, dwarfed by an urban landscape of concrete, corrugated iron and tower blocks. The painter was an old friend, and he worked on a large preliminary study over several sessions, developing a finely detailed image that Clive says looked like 'the bashed-up physiognomy of some Renaissance prince with a side interest in prizefighting'.

'He has a terribly strange face,' Smart told an art critic in 1999. 'His eyes are slits, so deep-set you cannot get any light into them.

His cheekbones are not on the same level, one ear is tremendously higher than the other, his nose is bent, his mouth contorted, and he has an enormously thick neck. I painted several studies of Clive, each one smaller than the previous one, until I'd got him down to the size of a postage stamp.'

In the end, Smart's artistic vision of the composition as a whole overruled his fascination with his subject's facial features. The finished painting, 'Portrait of Clive James', now on permanent display in Sydney's Art Gallery of New South Wales, places Clive way off in the middle distance, his face so small as to be virtually unrecognisable.

'He gave us the study for my portrait,' Clive wrote twenty years later. 'It is still with us in Cambridge, a noble head betraying no hint that its destiny is to be hit by a death ray that will shrink it to the size of a lemon.'

Raphael and Smart painted Clive in the early 1990s, and he never forgot the strange, dislocating experience of being seen through another's eyes. He came back to it many years later, in a short poem that neatly captures both the narcissist's desire to see his inner beauty shining through and the impostor's fear that he will be exposed in all his naked insecurity by the artist's X-ray vision.

The setting for 'Portrait of Man Writing' is a portrait session in which an older man is being painted by a young artist. As he sits for the painting, he marvels at the twenty-four-year-old woman's youthful skin and the beauty of her lips and eyelashes. But even as he watches her at work, he has to recognise the limitations of his own art. If he, as a writer, tried to describe these things as he sees them, the words would come out sounding like mere clichés. In this sense, painting has the edge on poetry. She can paint her subject as he is, with unflinching fidelity to what she sees in front of her. Indeed, she has no choice: 'You've got integrity like a disease. / Bound to record the damage of the years, / You aim to tell the truth, and not to please.' He would like her painting to capture the echo of his past vitality – the mouth that once had 'the knack for spinning yarns and casting spells', the eyes that 'once keenly shone'. But she must paint the present, not the past. A portrait is a snapshot, fixed in time, however long the shutter takes to click. His silent hope, that this picture, painted in 2005, will show 'at least a glimmer of what's gone', is doomed to disappointment.

The reflexive nature of this situation obviously intrigued Clive. Like Van Gogh painting himself painting, the writer is primarily writing about himself writing. The poem is, after all, called 'Portrait of Man Writing', and the woman painter is idealised, rather than individualised. But the setting is plausibly naturalistic. The morning passes without the sitter seeing the image that is taking shape on the far side of the canvas, and his impatience to know what the artist has made of him leads to a brilliantly conceived final payoff. We all have a romanticised picture of ourselves, and the portrait painter's view seldom coincides with that.

When the moment of revelation comes, it is almost bound to be a disappointment, one way or another. If the portrait is flattering, we know it is not true. If it strikes us as true, it is hardly likely to be flattering. True and unflattering is better, but this truth is hard to swallow. And that's what we get at the end of the poem, summed up

in a poignant snatch of one-sided dialogue: 'Let's break for lunch.
What progress have we made? / Ah yes. That's me exactly, I'm afraid.'

Portrait of Man Writing

While you paint me, I marvel at your skin.
The miracle of being twenty-four
Is there like a first blush as you touch in
The blemishes that make my face a war
I'm losing against time. So you begin,
By lending inwardness to an outline,
Your life in art as I am ending mine.

Try not to miss the story my mouth tells,
Even unmoving, of how once it had
The knack for spinning yarns and casting spells,
And had to make an effort to seem sad.
These eyes that look as crusty as dry wells
Despite the glue they seep, once keenly shone.
Give them at least a glimmer of what's gone.

I know these silent prayers fall on deaf ears:
You've got integrity like a disease.
Bound to record the damage of the years,
You aim to tell the truth, and not to please.
And so this other man slowly appears
Who is not me as I would wish to be,
But is the me that I try not to see.

Suppose while you paint me I wrote of you
With the same fidelity: people would say
That not a line could possibly be true.
Nobody's lips in real life glow that way.
Silk eyelashes! Is this what he's come to?
Your portrait, put in words, sounds like a lie,
Minus the facts a glance would verify.

But do we credit beauty even when
It's there in front of us? It stops the heart.
The mortal clockwork has to start again,
Ticking towards the day we fall apart,
Before we see now all we won't have then.
Let's break for lunch. What progress have we made?
Ah yes. That's me exactly, I'm afraid.

9

1815 and All That

When I was young, just twelve years old, I sat at my great-grandmother's bedside and talked with her about her own childhood. Her name was Eleanor Parkman. She was 101, born in 1859, the year of Darwin's *On the Origin of Species* and Dickens's *A Tale of Two Cities*, and she'd had her telegram from the Queen the year before. I realised, even as I held her hand in her last illness, that she could tell me stuff I would never hear from anyone else.

'What's the earliest thing you can remember, Gran?' I asked.

She told me about going to school, about sitting at an iron-framed desk in a bleak, unlit schoolroom heated by a coal stove, writing line after line of As and Bs with a stick of chalk on a wooden-framed slate board. She told me about a world of clay pipes and gas lights, turnpike barriers across the roads and people walking everywhere (no cars, of course, but no bicycles either, till the 1880s). She told me about the hottest summer for a hundred years, when she was nine, when the temperature where she lived, near Tonbridge, in Kent, was more than 100 degrees (38° Celsius). But I wanted more.

'Well,' she said. 'There is something else. I was curious when I was young, like you are now. I remember asking my grandmother the question you just asked me: what was the earliest thing she remembered?'

'And what did she say?'

'She said: "Ah, yes. I remember the riders clattering through the town, standing tall in their stirrups and shouting the news of the great victory. The French had been beaten, and England was safe again." That was her earliest memory.'

Waterloo. 1815. I was talking to someone I knew and loved who had talked to someone who was a girl when Napoleon was defeated. For a few seconds, the past opened up in front of me and I felt a direct, personal link right back to pre-Victorian, pre-Industrial Revolution, pre-everything England. It took my breath away, like vertigo. That glimpse down the hollow well of history was a feeling that would stay with me for ever.

In terms of the history of English poetry, the leap back to 1815 feels even more remarkable. Byron had not met Shelley. Keats hadn't seen a single poem of his in print. Browning and Edward Lear were toddlers. And Coleridge was finally getting round to the idea that 'Kubla Khan', which he'd written in 1797, would never actually be completed and might as well be published as an unfinished fragment.

For most of us, history ends abruptly on the day we were born. After that, it's now, modern times, the present.

I was born in October 1948, so India's independence and the founding of the National Health Service are history for me, whereas the Festival of Britain, sweet rationing, the Coronation, the conquest of Everest, Roger Bannister's four-minute mile, compulsory National Service and the first Comet jet airliners are all part of my present, along with Bill Haley, *My Fair Lady*, Elvis Presley and The Beatles. If you were born in the seventies or the eighties, all of those will feel like historical events, not all that different from the two world wars, the Great Depression or the publication of *Ulysses* or *The Waste Land*. The throwaway phrase 'before my time' means just what it says. So the fact that I have spent many hours talking, as a child, to an elderly relative who, in her turn, had talked to someone who was alive at the time of Waterloo still seems extraordinary to me. The telescoping of history that takes me back to 1815 in a couple of jumps is something I have never forgotten.

When Clive James had a flash of the same kind of feeling, while he was talking at dinner to Lady Diana Cooper, the eccentric aristocrat who had once been the most beautiful woman in Britain, but now, at ninety, was getting past her prime, he made a poem out of it, entitled 'Six Degrees of Separation from Shelley'.

Lady Diana, the mother of the historian and broadcaster John Julius Norwich, had enjoyed a rich and interesting life. Before World War I she had, as Clive records in *The Blaze of Obscurity*, been shooting heroin 'in quantities that would have impressed Keith Richards' and she was adored by every gentleman in London. Her fragile charms and provocative chastity had broken a dozen hearts, and, after the war, when all but one of her suitors had died, she married the lucky survivor, Alfred Duff Cooper. She then turned to acting, under her maiden name, Diana Manners, becoming a star of the silent screen and a huge success on Broadway. She had been the leading light of London society throughout the twenties and thirties and on into the forties, when the industriously promiscuous Duff Cooper became the British Ambassador in newly liberated Paris and the golden couple held the most dazzling and extravagant soirées in town.

In her later years, the spotlight had shifted elsewhere, but she was still witty (she would introduce herself to people, in the early 1980s, as 'the wrong Lady Diana'), charismatic and monstrously confident. She was also bluntly opinionated (she did actually assert that all the poor people should be killed – 'After all, we *are* the *best people*') and full of a lifetime's worth of stories about the great and the good and the very, very bad.

Lady Diana's advanced age and vivid recollections obviously set Clive's magpie memory going. When she was little, as a girl of eleven or twelve, she had known the poet and novelist George Meredith, who had given her a signed copy of *Modern Love*, his book of fifty poems about the failure of his first marriage. His wife, who had run off with a pre-Raphaelite painter, was the daughter of the satirical novelist Thomas Love Peacock. And Peacock was a close friend of Percy Bysshe Shelley – so close, in fact, that he is said to have saved the ailing Shelley's life. They were on a trip up the Thames together, in 1815, when the great Romantic collapsed as a result of living on a narrow and inadequate vegetarian diet – 'chiefly on tea and bread and butter', according to Peacock.

Historians disagree about whether it was a steak or, as some say, 'three mutton chops, well peppered', that his friend waved under Shelley's nose. Whatever it was, though, it did the trick. The veggie poet ate the meat, recovered his health and lived to write

'Ozymandias', 'Ode to the West Wind', 'To a Skylark' and *Prometheus Unbound*, among much else.

The elements in this chain of connections, history-hopping back from Lady Diana Cooper to George Meredith and from Meredith, via Mary Ellen Peacock, to Thomas Love Peacock and the wilting vegetarian, had obviously been lurking somewhere in the back of Clive's mind. And since picking up on unlikely associations had always been part of his stock in trade, it's not surprising that he wrote a poem establishing his own almost intimate connection with Shelley. The idea that everyone in the world could be shown to be no more than six degrees of separation from anyone else was in the air at that time – a popular buzz-phrase that led to a high-profile movie a few years later, starring Will Smith and Donald Sutherland. The links were supposed to be geographical, rather than historical, but it's easy to see why Clive found the idea of tracing a cultural family tree back to the time of Waterloo irresistible.

Whether the poem works, in its own terms, is more questionable. In one sense, it is the most prosaic poem you are ever likely to come across. The use of completely conventional syntax, punctuation and phrasing means that it can easily be read as prose – dense and packed with ideas, full of unexpected detail and graphic images, but arguably no more poetic in its form than many passages from Clive's newspaper journalism or the startlingly eclectic essays in his prose masterwork, *Cultural Amnesia*. What is clear is that there is a considerable change of pace and focus after the opening four stanzas, which are mainly concerned with outlining the sequence of connections leading back to 1815. The remaining two are different, first in setting up Shelley's blazing revolutionary fervour – with the suggestion that he might think the rich should be killed off – and then in suggesting that the gleam of his funeral pyre might be seen in Lady Diana's eyes as she swept into her nineties, still so full of life that she had no use for the poison she had carried with her for decades. This famously deadly phial, reserved for the day when everything eventually became too much, or too little, to bear, becomes a symbol of her irrepressible spirit. Like Shelley, she is driven by passions beyond the rational. And Clive, who, with Shelley, is opposed to almost everything she has ever stood for, politically and socially, can only admire her tenacity and hope that he, too, will never want to reach for the poison.

In terms of its subject matter, 'Six Degrees of Separation from Shelley' could fit in quite neatly among the poems of Clive's last few disease-stricken years, though it was actually written when he was in his early forties. The effective contrast between Diana Cooper's right-wing extremism ('kill the poor') and Shelley's presumed view ('kill the rich') gives them each a fanatical edge, though Lady Manners was predictably famed for her courtesy and the tender-hearted poet could not usually bring himself to eat the flesh of any animal. If both of them really believed the world could be made better by the mass slaughter of a substantial section of the population, neither could be in the right. But both, Clive seems to be saying, possessed some essential life force that is ultimately important and valuable.

On first reading, 'Six Degrees of Separation from Shelley' may seem little more than a juggling trick, as light and insubstantial as

1927's novelty hit 'I've Danced with a Man Who's Danced with a Girl Who's Danced with the Prince of Wales'. I think it's more than that. There are dark undercurrents here, quite apart from the elements of class warfare. Clive's references to Ernest Dowson and Lewis Carroll play no functional role in his mapping of the chain of connections back to Shelley, but they are not there by chance. Dowson, creator of such magnificent movie-title phrases as 'the days of wine and roses' and 'gone with the wind', was the very model of a dissolute bohemian consumptive, though TS Eliot called him 'the most gifted and technically perfect poet of his age'. Carroll was, well, Carroll – a strange, tortured and totally original genius. But what links them, and brings them together in Clive's poem, is the inescapable whiff of paedophilia that surrounds them both. The heated discussion about the nature of Carroll's interest in Alice Liddell may never be wholly resolved, but there is no doubt about Dowson's long-standing infatuation with his 'little Polish demoiselle', Adelaide Foltinowicz, which began when the girl was just eleven years old.

'Six Degrees of Separation from Shelley' is about life, sex and death. When Shelley's drowned body was cremated on the beach in Italy, his friend, Edward Trelawny, apparently plunged his hand into the embers and retrieved the unburned heart, creating a potent symbol of survival beyond the grave. Clive does not mention this directly, but he does claim to see the light from the poet's funeral pyre reflected in Lady Diana Cooper's eyes as she moves towards the end of her own life, nearly 170 years later, with her phial of poison still intact. In the end, the life force wins, by the narrowest of margins. The prejudices, the passions, the vanity and the egocentricities that link the Romantic poet and the aristocratic dowager are not quite enough to snuff it out. Diana Cooper says the poor would be better dead, but 'I think her tongue was in her cheek'. Shelley would have wanted the rich killed, 'probably'. The 'probably' and the 'I think' leave room for just enough uncertainty. And the fact that the poison kept 'against the day there was nothing left to live for' has never been used reassures us that there are always reasons to keep going, even when, as in Lady Diana Cooper's case, the world has changed and moved on around you.

Six Degrees of Separation from Shelley

In the last year of her life I dined with Diana Cooper
Who told me she thought the best thing to do with the poor
Was to kill them. I think her tongue was in her cheek
But with that much plastic surgery it was hard to tell.

As a child she had sat on the knee of George Meredith,
More than forty years after he published *Modern Love*.
Though she must have been as pretty as any poppet
Who challenged the trousers of Dowson or Lewis Carroll,

We can bet Meredith wasn't as modern as that.
By then the old boy wouldn't have felt a twinge
Even had he foreseen she would one day arrive
In Paris with an escort of two dozen Spitfires.

The book lamented his marriage to one of the daughters
Of Peacock. Peacock when young rescued Shelley
From a coma brought on through an excess of vegetarianism
By waving a steak under his sensitive nose.

Shelley never quite said that the best thing to do with the rich
Was to kill them, but he probably thought so.
Whether the steak was cooked or raw I can't remember.
I should, of course. I was practically there:

The blaze of his funeral pyre on the beach at night
Was still in her eyes. At her age I hope to recall
The phial of poison she carried but never used
Against the day there was nothing left to live for.

10

At Ian Hamilton's Funeral

Philip Larkin – a great poet, for all his controversial flaws and failings as a man, and the subject of Clive's 2019 book, *Somewhere Becoming Rain* – knew exactly what he wanted to do each time he sat down to write. He understood what poetry can do that other art forms cannot achieve and he summed it up beautifully. His aim, he once said, was 'to construct a verbal device that would preserve an experience indefinitely by reproducing it in whoever read the poem'.

That was in 1964, and he backtracked on it almost immediately, dismissing this fine 'working definition' of his ambitions as 'oversimplified'. But there is something truly exciting and provocative about the idea that poetry recreates experience, rather than merely depicting or reporting it. For me, Larkin's comment links up with an insight put forward forty years later by Don Paterson, when he gave the 2004 TS Eliot Lecture.

'A poem is just a little machine for remembering itself,' he told his audience at the Poetry International festival in London. 'The one unique thing about our art is that it can be carried around in your head in its original state, intact and perfect. We merely *recall* a string quartet, or a film, or a painting – actually, at a neurological level, we're only remembering a memory of it. But our memory of the poem *is* the poem.

'Prose evokes; the well-chosen word describes the thing. But poetry *invokes*; the memorable word conjures its subject from the air.'

Paterson is a marvellous poet in his own right, as well as being a smart and incisive critic, the man who has built Picador's poetry list and the editor Clive James has worked with on his poetry collections for more than twenty years. Like Clive, he writes speakable, accessible poems, meticulously worked but full of twists and surprises, tenderness and satire, drama and humour. He likes to take risks, and sometimes he'll go too far. There is a Don Paterson poem called 'On Going to Meet a Zen Master in the Kyushu Mountains and Not Finding Him' that I am going to quote in full here, despite not having obtained permission. Here is the entire text that follows the title:

That was it. You may have liked it, or maybe not. But if that was not to your taste, you should look up his sonnet, 'Mercies', a restrained and heartbreaking description of that awful moment when you have to take a much-loved dog to the vet for the last time. In terms of scope and scale, Paterson and James are soulmates, and the working relationship between them has been stimulating and productive, though Clive pretends to be intimidated by the younger man's rigour and certainty.

'If Paterson had his way,' he told me, 'nothing I published would be longer than four lines. He believes in discipline. Mainly for me, of course – not so much for him.'

Needless to say, that's not true. Paterson has a particular soft spot for Clive's longest poems, *Peregrine Prykke's Pilgrimage*, *Felicity Fark* and *Britannia Bright*, all written in the mid-1970s, and *Charles Charming*, which dates from 1981. He is already toying with the idea of persuading Picador to republish all four of them, despite the inevitable erosion of their topical relevance by the decades that have passed since they first saw the light of day. But his assertion that a poem is just a machine for remembering itself can't possibly be true for such sprawling epics, any more than it could be for *Paradise Lost* or *The Rime of the Ancient Mariner*, or *The Waste Land* or Ginsberg's *Howl*. Beyond a certain length, the memory just gives up. So the machine-for-remembering-itself idea is mostly applicable to short lyric poems. That may be why, with Don Paterson at his elbow, the poems Clive has published in the last twenty years, apart from *The River in the Sky*, have generally been pared down to a few succinct verses.

The exceptions, though, tend to be serious and ambitious works that tackle subjects too complex to be handled with his usual brevity. And one of the most moving and fully realised is his elegy on the death of his friend, mentor and editor, Ian Hamilton. It is a long poem, too long to be reproduced in full in this book, but its thirteen eight-line stanzas will send chills of recognition down the spine of anyone who has suffered a similar loss.

'At Ian Hamilton's Funeral' conjures up the grief, the disbelief, the ambiguities and contradictions, the sense of shared bereavement and even the flickerings of survivor's guilt that ripple through such occasions. It notes the cynicism the non-religious feel about comforting promises of an afterlife, and the way perspectives shift and disconnected thoughts crowd the mind as a mixed assembly of friends and strangers slowly merges into a unified and grieving congregation. The feelings are familiar to most of us, but the viewpoint is entirely Clive's. From his private musings as he makes his preparations to the numbed pause before the event begins, the arrival of the hearse, the flood of personal memories, the grim, solemn ceremony itself, the eulogies, the committal and the hushed conversations as the mourners emerge into the winter sunlight, he takes us through a succession of scenes that seem as powerful and specific as any film.

Ian Hamilton died in 2001. He was a talented and pitiless editor, a highly readable reviewer and biographer and a severely minimalist poet. In forty years he wrote just sixty poems, few of them more than a dozen lines long, with only one that runs to more than a page. He was also an ardent Spurs fan, a heavy smoker and a relentless drinker, famous for his dry humour, his bailiff-haunted financial scrapes and his chaotic love life. He founded two highly influential literary magazines, first the *Review*, which lasted ten years, and later the *New Review*, which was sustained for five years by subsidies from the Arts Council, personal loans and the efforts of a bevy of earnest young women who worked night and day to keep the wheels turning. His passion and charisma were magnetic. Contributors would waive their fees for the good of the cause and the upper-class girls in the office often worked for love when the money ran out.

'We all slept with him, of course,' one of these editorial elves said years later. 'Anyone who tells you they didn't is a liar.'

Hamilton inspired devotion in men as well as women, and his eye for new talent was legendary. The tight (and noticeably male) group of writers, reviewers and poets he gathered around him included Ian McEwan and Julian Barnes, Martin Amis and Craig Raine, Christopher Hitchens and Russell Davies, Andrew Motion and, of course, Clive James. Both the posh girls and the men of letters are there in the poem, all remembering the dead man in their own private ways:

> The London literati take
> Their places pew to pew and aisle to aisle
> At murmured random. Nothing is at stake
> Except the recollection of your smile.
> All earned it. Who most often? For your sake
> Men wrote all night, and as for women, well,
> How many of them loved you none can tell.
>
> Those who are here among us wear the years
> With ease, as fine-boned beauty tends to do.
> It wasn't just your looks that won the tears
> That spill today when they remember you.
> Most of us had our minds on our careers.
> You were our conscience, and your women knew
> Just by our deference the man in black
> Who said least was the leader of the pack.

This is fine, minutely observed stuff. The writers who take their places 'pew to pew and aisle to aisle at murmured random' are doing exactly what we all tend to do at funerals, where no-one wants to be at the front and no-one feels that sitting at the very back is right either. Once seated, people look around and begin to notice those near them, remembering who's who, updating faces, and, in this case, registering the way that 'fine-boned beauty' is able to 'wear the years with ease'. Yet in this atmosphere of hushed solemnity, odd and unexpected thoughts and associations keep breaking through.

Ian Hamilton often wore black ('dressed all your life for mourning'). To a poet with a head full of songs, that links him to Johnny Cash, known for decades as The Man in Black. Hamilton was, as the poem says later, 'the governor, the chief, the squire'. Now he's gone, and Clive can't help thinking of the Shangri-Las 'Leader of the Pack', a 1960s 'splatter platter' melodrama sung by a schoolgirl whose rejected boyfriend has roared off and died in a motorcycle accident.

'Extraordinary,' says Noël Coward's Amanda in *Private Lives*, 'how potent cheap music is.' And how intrusive. On this strange and mournful day, it floods in, filling the cracks and insinuating itself where it has no business to be. Indeed, right back in the first stanza, when Clive is alone, fumbling with his black tie, his nostalgia for the camaraderie within the little group that gathered around Hamilton in the pubs of Soho makes him think of a sentimental song from the 1920s, 'The Gang That Sang "Heart of My Heart"', which was revived in the early 1950s and became a hit for both The Four Aces and the inexplicably popular Max Bygraves. The members of his own gang have gone their separate ways over the years, and it takes the funeral service to reunite them: 'Death brings together what time pulled apart.'

The five stanzas that describe Hamilton and the Soho scene that revolved around him, the *New Review*'s office and the Pillars of Hercules pub, three doors away, are remarkable in their evocative detail. They describe Hamilton's donnish attitude towards his authors

('While you read his manuscript / You gave its perpetrator time to think / Of taking up another trade. White-lipped / He watched you sneer. But sometimes you would blink / Or nod or even chuckle while you sipped'). They recall old disagreements, such as a running quarrel about the pros and cons of Robert Frost (his 'folksy pomp and circumstance' offset by moments of 'pure expression'). They record Clive's own delight when 'my sideshow razzmatazz you rarely blessed' struck home and wrung a 'reluctant grin' from the fastidious editor. And they emphasise the warmth and wit that made it all worth while and led these pushy up-and-coming talents to feel protective of their brilliant but unworldly and strangely vulnerable mentor.

All this has been written about many times, not least in Clive's own book, *North Face of Soho*, the fourth volume of his *Unreliable Memoirs* sequence. Each of the members of the charmed circle knew it was a privilege to be there, but each saw the situation slightly differently. Ian McEwan, for example, didn't subscribe to the view of Hamilton as 'literature's flinty enforcer' – he thought of him as 'pleasant, even avuncular' – but he did admit he was hard to impress.

'Ian was the sort of editor writers wanted to please,' wrote McEwan. 'He didn't hand out praise, or even condemnation; it was silence, neither lofty nor benign, more a kind of butch restraint, that worked the trick.'

He doesn't deny the 'dram of truth' in accusations that the *New Review* was 'an excuse for a piss-up', but points out that 'the writing and editing got done, and to the highest standards'. The friendships, the drinking, the competitiveness and the sparring were all part of the milieu Hamilton created, and the writers all 'felt flattered to be included'.

The memories are poignant, personal and painful. Throughout this poem, there are superbly terse lines that capture the unspoken thoughts of those who wait to say their goodbyes. When the hearse draws up, it's impossible not to look, but equally impossible to imagine that all that's left of a beloved friend is fitted inside so small a coffin: 'No-one would call the centre of the scene / That little box inside the big black car.' When the casket is carried down the aisle, the dam breaks, the heart 'heaves' (a wrenchingly accurate description) and the bitter truth of death hits home.

> Laughter in life, and dark, unsmiling art:
> There lay, or seemed to lie, the paradox.
> Which was the spirit, which the mortal part?
> As if in answer, borne aloft, the box
> Goes by one slow step at a time. The heart
> At last heaves and the reservoir unlocks
> Of sorrow. That was you, and you are gone
> First to the altar, then to oblivion.

The ironies of the situation are summed up with piercing clarity: 'You lie straight and hidden, very near / Yet just as far off as the other dead.' Hamilton did not believe in the possibility of life after death, yet his friends, filing quietly out of the church, console themselves with the thought that something of his spirit lives on in their memories and their love.

'At Ian Hamilton's Funeral' is simply too long to be known by heart, so it doesn't qualify as one of Don Paterson's little machines for remembering itself. It does, though, provide a fine example of what Philip Larkin meant when he talked about 'a verbal device that would preserve an experience indefinitely by reproducing it in whoever read the poem'. For those of us who have known the loss of loved ones and the strange ceremonial of the funeral rites, it is genuinely an evocation, rather than a description, triggering our own memories and vividly reactivating the feelings we have lived through. Written nearly two decades ago, before Clive's own precarious mortality had elbowed itself into the foreground of his consciousness, it shows him at his best, both as an observer and a poet.

In fact, though, he has always been good at death. And this is not the first time he has tackled the rituals and symbolism associated with funerals – so similar in their fundamentals across classes and generations, so subtly differentiated in their forms and formalities. Way back in the early seventies, one of his most memorable collaborations with Pete Atkin was an angry song called 'Carnations on the Roof', about the funeral and cremation of an industrial sheet metal worker. Originally written to be a poem, before Clive realised he had a song lyric on his hands, it includes one dazzling and strikingly original image. As the flames engulf the dead man's body, the metal filings that have impregnated his skin during a lifetime at the workbench burn with a glittering, pyrotechnic blaze of colour – orange for iron, white for aluminium, blue for copper. Clive's treasure house of two hundred extraordinary song lyrics, written with Atkin over nearly half a century, still remains largely undiscovered, but it is well worth taking three minutes or so to find 'Carnations on the Roof' on YouTube. The working-class funeral depicted here is very different from the urbane gathering of literary minds at Ian Hamilton's send-off, but both the poem and the song show a more sensitive and finely calibrated Clive James than his public career might lead new readers to expect.

Clive has always been proud of 'At Ian Hamilton's Funeral', both for its content and its technical polish. The poem is classical in form, written in iambic pentameters and using the same strict ABABABCC *ottava rima* rhyme scheme as Byron's epic *Don Juan* and Yeats's 'Sailing to Byzantium'. But the man's a craftsman, and he finds plenty of opportunities within this framework to capture the sway and shift of natural, conversational rhythms, marshalling the breaks within the lines to play against the apparent rigidity of the form: 'The body-blow / You dealt us when you left we will believe / When it sinks in. We haven't let you go / As yet. Outside the church, you're here with us. / Whatever's said, it's you that we discuss.' At the same time, the majestic power of the rhymed iambic pentameters lends itself to moments of solid grandeur. It's there early on, in the first three lines of the second stanza: 'In Wimbledon, a cold bright New Year's Eve / Shines on the faces that you used to know / But only lights the depth to which they grieve'. And it builds beautifully, in the poem's last lines, to a monumental ending worthy of Marvell or Donne: 'The awareness of love, how it defends / Itself against forgetfulness, and gives / Through death the best assurance that it lives'.

When critics accuse Clive of being an old-fashioned Formalist, hampered in his ability to express himself by his voluntary subjection to traditional rhyme and metre, this is one example he would cite as proof that discipline needn't exclude feeling.

'It was a big day,' he says. 'This is an elegy for someone who was important to me, and I'm still fond of it. It's one of the poems I would wave at people who say my poetry is artificially restricted by its formal requirements. They accuse me of distorting my syntax and phrasing in the service of a formal framework, but that doesn't necessarily happen. And you can't do everything as if you're proving you can do it. Sometimes you just want to do it that way.'

At Ian Hamilton's Funeral (excerpt)

Dressed all your life for mourning, you made no
Display. Although your prose was eloquent,
Your poetry fought shy of outward show.
Pain and regret said no more than they meant.
Love sued for peace but had nowhere to go.
Joy was a book advance already spent,
And yet by day, free from the soul's midnight,
Your conversation was a sheer delight.

Thirsty for more of it, we came to drink
In Soho. While you read his manuscript
You gave its perpetrator time to think
Of taking up another trade. White-lipped
He watched you sneer. But sometimes you would blink
Or nod or even chuckle while you sipped
Your Scotch, and then came the acceptance fee:
The wit, the gossip, the hilarity.

You paid us from your only source of wealth.
Your finances were always in a mess.
We told each other we did good by stealth.
In private we took pride in a success:
Knowing the way of life that wrecked your health
Was death-defying faith, not fecklessness,
We preened to feel your hard-won lack of guile
Rub off on us for just a little while.

For lyric truth, such suffering is the cost –
So the equation goes you incarnated.
The rest of us must ponder what we lost
When we so prudently equivocated.
But you yourself had time for Robert Frost –
His folksy pomp and circumstance you hated,
Yet loved his moments of that pure expression
You made your own sole aim if not obsession.

Our quarrel about that's not over yet,
But here today we have to let it rest.
The disagreements we could not forget
In life will fade now and it's for the best.
Your work was a sad trumpet at sunset.
My sideshow razzmatazz you rarely blessed
Except with the reluctant grin I treasured
The most of all the ways my stuff was measured.

Laughter in life, and dark, unsmiling art:
There lay, or seemed to lie, the paradox.

Which was the spirit, which the mortal part?
As if in answer, borne aloft, the box
Goes by one slow step at a time. The heart
At last heaves and the reservoir unlocks
Of sorrow. That was you, and you are gone:
First to the altar, then to oblivion.

The rest is ceremony, and well said.
Your brother speaks what you would blush to hear
Were you alive and standing with bowed head.
But you lie straight and hidden, very near
Yet just as far off as the other dead
Each of us knows will never reappear.
You were the governor, the chief, the squire,
And now what's left of you leaves for the fire.

Ashes will breed no phoenix, you were sure
Of that, but not right. You should hear your friends
Who rise to follow, and outside the door
Agree this is a sad day yet it ends
In something that was not so clear before:
The awareness of love, how it defends
Itself against forgetfulness, and gives
Through death the best assurance that it lives.

11

Dream Me Some Happiness

In a previous book, about his song lyrics, I mentioned the parallels I saw between Clive's boisterously inventive approach to his craft and that of John Donne. But James and Donne, four hundred years apart, are linked by more than just a taste for vigorous wordplay and unexpected metaphors.

The Reverend John Donne, Dean of St Paul's, Catholic turned Protestant by the pressure of the times, wrote some marvellous satirical and religious poetry. But his great passion was for life, for love and for women. His short poems reek with the pungent scent of lust and hum with the heat of urgent desire. They are some of the most powerfully sensual and seductive verses ever written in English, and it is easy to forget that almost all of them were only published for the first time – in an unauthorised pirate edition – in 1633, two years after his death.

If his greatest poems stemmed from his early life as 'a great visiter of ladies, a great frequenter of playes, a great writer of conceited verses', as one contemporary chronicler described him, there were no printed books to prove the point and taint the dean's holy reputation. The early songs and sonnets had been passed round among Donne's friends in manuscript form, along with strict orders not to make copies of them, because of what he referred to as his 'fear' and 'perhaps shame' at the thought of such material being made public. How much difference his instructions made is questionable, as there are still, even now, more than 5000 surviving hand-copied versions of his individual poems, most of them dating from the early seventeenth century.

For Clive, John Donne is as great as an English poet can be without being Shakespeare. He talks of him as 'my touchstone poet' and regards him as a vital, practical influence – not just appreciated as a historical giant, but drawn on directly as a source of energy and inspiration.

'Donne lives in my mind almost every day as I sit down to write,' he said, in one of his fascinating Australian radio conversations with his friend and fellow expat poet Peter Porter, recorded in 2000. Donne's conversational tone, good humour, fondness for topical references and delight in the exercise of his craft all find echoes in the best of Clive's writing, from his essays and TV criticism to his *Unreliable Memoirs* and nearly sixty years of poetry. But there is also a knowing worldliness that reaches down across the centuries and links the two men.

Donne's life story was extraordinary. His father died when he was three. His mother was a great-niece of the martyred Sir Thomas More, author of *Utopia* and Henry VIII's Lord Chancellor for four years, who, as a Catholic, refused to support his king against the Pope and was beheaded for treason. Donne's beloved younger brother, Henry, a student, was cruelly tortured until he confessed to harbouring a Papist priest. He was thrown into Newgate Prison, where he died of the plague, at the age of nineteen. By his mid-twenties, Donne had studied for three years at Oxford and three at Cambridge, qualified as a lawyer at the Inns of Court, fought alongside Essex and Raleigh against the Spanish at Cádiz and in the Azores, spent years in Italy and Spain, learning both languages, and got himself a plum job as secretary to the Lord Keeper of the Great Seal, placing him right at the heart of political life in London.

He then blew it all by marrying his beloved Anne against the wishes of her family, which led to him being sacked and thrown into the Fleet Prison, along with the priest who married them and even the man who witnessed their wedding vows.

On his release, Donne became an MP (an unpaid job at that time) and struggled to make ends meet, working as a lawyer and freelancing as an anti-Catholic pamphleteer, while Anne bore him twelve children in sixteen years, including two stillborn babies. Of those who survived, three died before the age of ten, plunging him into suicidal despair. When he eventually found his feet, his religious poetry attracted the attention of the king, James I, who repeatedly urged him to become ordained in the Church of England. Donne gave way, eventually, and was appointed a royal chaplain. But his wife died and Donne spent two years on a diplomatic mission to Germany before being appointed Dean of St Paul's, where he became an honoured and well-paid member of the establishment.

In his poem 'Dream Me Some Happiness', Clive sets Donne's conversion in the context of the grim realities of a fretful and rabidly anti-Catholic state. The authorities were tireless and conscientious in signalling their determination to deal with dissidents, employing a great deal of crushing, racking, gouging and dismemberment to put their point across. (When the Gunpowder Plot was uncovered, it was stipulated in court that Guy Fawkes and his Catholic fellow-conspirators should have their genitals cut off and burned before their eyes before they enjoyed the relief of being hanged, disembowelled, beheaded and quartered.) The crown persecution service, led, in the later years of Elizabeth's reign, by the brutal torturer Richard Topcliffe, was everywhere. The poem's 'tangles of gristle, relics of hair and bone' were all too real and all too familiar, images as powerful and unforgettable, in their own way, as Donne's own 'heterogeneous ideas... yoked by violence together'.

For Clive, an unmistakably metaphysical poet himself, in terms of the outrageous verve and eclecticism of his conceits, contemplation of Donne's religious compromises leads directly to this poem's focal point, the idea of 'bad faith'. The double-edged phrase obviously applies both to Donne's negotiated settlement with his soul in the matter of religion and to his attitude to the women in whom he takes such ecstatic delight.

Clive is well aware of the way his hero's reputation has waxed and waned over the years. Adored in the seventeenth century, reviled in the eighteenth and forgotten in the nineteenth, Donne became enormously popular in the mid-twentieth, when sex was reinvented ('in nineteen sixty-three', as Larkin reminded us) and his bold imagery and wordplay caught the mood of the times. Since then, opinions have been more mixed, with academic critics coming at the poems from all kinds of different viewpoints – linguistic, psychobiographical, historicist, formalistic and, above all, feminist – and often blaming the 400-year-old poet for not being more in tune with modern thinking.

Clive's view of John Donne's poems is overwhelmingly positive. He has no problem with Donne's enthusiastic eroticism, his love of puns and paradox, or his willingness to bend the metrical rules to make a line twist and pulse the way he wanted ('The knotty strength that made him hard to scan'). This drive towards natural speech rhythms seems like a welcome progression to us now, and a direct response to what was happening in London's theatres, but many of his contemporaries found it maddening. Ben Jonson, who called him 'the first poet in the world in some things', felt he took unpardonable liberties with metre: 'Donne,' he said, 'for not keeping of accent, deserved hanging.'

Nor is Clive put off by the uncomfortably compromising pragmatism that led to Donne's religious conversion ('uneasiest of apostates', he calls him). The man had to live – whether that meant making a career or merely avoiding a premature end – and the dramatic and often traumatic events of his early life must have made him well aware of the fragility of human existence.

The title 'Dream Me Some Happiness' is taken from one of Donne's elegies, the one that begins 'By our first strange and fatal interview'. The numbering of these elegies is often confused, and the internet throws up hundreds of examples where this one is confidently labelled Elegy XVI or even Elegy XVII. Most Donne specialists, though, including the authors of the exhaustive and dizzyingly detailed *Variorum Edition of the Poetry of John Donne*, have settled on referring to it as Elegy 11.

It's a strange poem. Apparently addressed to his wife, Anne, at a time when Donne was about to set off on a lengthy jaunt across Europe, its main purpose seems to be to persuade her to prove the depth of her love by staying behind in England. He urges her not to do anything silly – like, for example, insisting on disguising herself as a boy and tagging along as his page, like some character in a Jacobean comedy. That wouldn't do any good at all, he says. The lecherous French would sniff her out at once and 'Th' indifferent Italian' – indifferent as to whether she was male or female – would 'hunt thee with such lust, and hideous rage' that it would be bound to end in tears.

But when the comedy is over, there is a serious point to be made. He doesn't want her having nightmares about terrible things happening to him.

> Nor in bed fright thy Nurse
> With midnight's startings, crying out – Oh, oh
> Nurse, O my love is slain. I saw him go
> O'er the white Alps alone; I saw him, I,
> Assailed, fight, taken, stabbed, bleed, fall, and die.

Leaving aside the extraordinarily graphic description of this agitated nightmare and the remarkable technical ingenuity with which Donne plays with the speech rhythms across his pentameter couplets and that last seven-verb line, this is about the power of dreams as auguries. He fears that if Anne dreams of disaster, the dream might come true. So she must help him by dreaming only of good things to come. 'When I am gone, dream me some happiness,' he says. 'Augur me better chance, except dread Jove / Think it enough for me t' have had thy love.'

Clive, of course, knows a good line when he sees one. He has the ear for it. With typical Jamesian opportunism, he purloined 'Dream me some happiness' as the title for his own poem about Donne, even though the phrase bore little direct relevance to the theme he was about to explore. He's done this sort of thing before. In one of his best early songs, 'Touch Has a Memory', he filched a line from Keats, made it the song's title and took it off in a completely different and unexpected direction as he mused on the relative durability of tactile memories, compared with our fading memories of sights and sounds.

'Dream Me Some Happiness' pivots on the idea of 'bad faith' ('Each kiss a Judas kiss, a double game'), gaily intertwining Donne's adaptable religious convictions with his ambivalent attitudes towards more earthly relationships. No-one has ever doubted Donne's ability to enchant both readers and potential lovers with his honeyed words, startling conceits and ingenious arguments. But it is impossible to ignore the fact that he – or at least the 'I' in his *Songs and Sonnets* – is prepared to cheat outrageously to get his own way and quite happy to blame his own promiscuity on his mistresses' loose morals.

There are plenty of examples of this in his love poems. 'Woman's Constancy', for example, wades straight in with the lines 'Now thou hast loved me one whole day, / Tomorrow when thou leav'st, what wilt thou say?' And 'The Indifferent' contains the notorious couplet

'I can love her, and her, and you, and you, / I can love any, so she be not true'.

The problem with Donne, however, is that the insistent urgency of physical desire in his love poetry readily persuades us that these poems are essentially autobiographical and written in the heat of the moment – almost as if they were penned right there, in the bedroom. That's unlikely, of course. The practicalities, at a time when pencils were not available and ink needed to be blotted with pounce (made of powdered cuttlefish bone) or sand to avoid smudging, would have made such spontaneity too difficult.

The assumption that these erotic masterpieces were accounts of the rakish poet's actual adventures, and that they were all written in his youth, before he met and married Anne, is equally unfounded. Dating Donne's poems is virtually impossible, and the subject of much scholarly debate, not least because only seven and a half of his poems were published in his lifetime. But there is no reason not to believe that they were works of imaginative fiction, with Donne consciously assuming different characters – sometimes romantic and tender, sometimes brutally cynical – for the purposes of each individual poem. Browning, after all, didn't murder duchesses. And the vindictively crowing voice we hear rejoicing in his rival's downfall in Clive's own hymn to literary schadenfreude, 'The Book of My Enemy Has Been Remaindered', does not necessarily represent Clive's true character.

Yet it remains almost impossible to avoid seeing the narrator of the love poems as Donne himself. However much we tell ourselves that the poem is not the poet, this is the John Donne we feel we know, the one voice of his era, other than Shakespeare's, that speaks to us across the centuries with such an abundance of energy, wit, humour and human fallibility. Like the enigmatic, comically anxious and paradoxically modern-seeming faces of the twelfth-century Lewis Chessmen, Donne's poems jolt us into the realisation that our distant ancestors were real flesh-and-blood people, much more like us than we generally assume. We *want* to think of the poems as autobiographical, because we *want* to know this man, with all his flaws and inconsistencies. In talking about the persona as if it were the man, Clive is only doing what every reader of Donne gets drawn into doing, including the many feminist critics for whom the *Songs and Sonnets* are a red rag to a bull.

In the second stanza of 'Dream Me Some Happiness', Clive levels the charge of hypocrisy at Donne, saying that he 'Ascribed his bad faith to his latest flame / As if the fact she could be bent to do / His bidding proved that she would not stay true'. Donne charms us, he says later, 'save in one respect: / Framing his women still looks like a crime'. But by the time we get to the last two stanzas, Clive is owning up to much the same offence.

We, too, 'foist our fault on her we claim to love', he says, even if we do it 'a different way'. Donne 'wrote betrayal into her delight', trying to blame his lover's appetites and kid himself that he bore no responsibility for the fact that this would be no more than a one night stand. That's not a line of reasoning that would cut much ice in our liberated and enlightened times. But the temptation to practise a modernised form of this self-deception is almost irresistible. Today it depends on a shared conspiracy to deny the realities of the situation.

I am fond of 'Dream Me Some Happiness', partly because, like Clive, I find Donne himself endlessly fascinating. I like the poem's neat, unobtrusive rhymes and the way the syntax moves from long, complex sentences, in the first five stanzas, to shorter, clipped statements as we accelerate towards the climax. There are phrases here – 'uneasiest of apostates', 'each kiss a Judas kiss', 'knotty strength', 'tangles of gristle, relics of hair and bone' – that have lodged in my mind for years.

Yet, at the same time, I can see that the poem is seriously flawed. For me, 'the mental muscle-man' is a distractingly leaden image. 'Not quite the Donne thing, when push comes to shove' seems doubly self-indulgent – a nudging, self-conscious line that should surely have been rethought. And I find it impossible to understand exactly what is going on in the last two stanzas. The implication seems to be that there is an element of collusion, with the lovers collaborating to deceive themselves ('as we help her help us believe / Life isn't like that') for a single night.

If this is a shared conspiracy, though, what is the reader supposed to make of the assertion that 'we have a better reason to deceive ourselves'? The 'we' here is clearly a substitute for 'one' or even 'I' (hence 'we help her help us believe'), but there's no clue as to what the 'better reason' might be. Donne is 'framing his women' to absolve himself from any responsibility for their actions, foisting his fault on those he claims to love. In 'Dream Me Some Happiness', the narrator confesses he's doing the same thing 'a different way'. But the 'different way', like the 'better reason', remains obscure. This is unlike Clive. I find it unsatisfyingly vague, rather than tantalisingly mysterious, especially at the end of a poem that has delivered many rich delights along the way.

Dream Me Some Happiness

John Donne, uneasiest of apostates,
Renouncing Rome that he might get ahead
In life, or anyway not wind up dead,
Minus his guts or pressed beneath great weights,

Ascribed his bad faith to his latest flame
As if the fact she could be bent to do
His bidding proved that she would not stay true:
Each kiss a Judas kiss, a double game.

Compared with him, the mental muscle-man,
Successors who declared his numbers rough
Revealed by theirs they found the pace too tough:
The knotty strength that made him hard to scan

Left him renowned for his conceits alone,
Figments unfading as the forms of death
Prescribed for Catholics by Elizabeth –
Tangles of gristle, relics of hair and bone.

Brought back to favour in an anxious time
Attuned to his tormented intellect,
By now he charms us, save in one respect:
Framing his women still looks like a crime.

We foist our fault on her we claim to love
A different way. Pleased to the point of tears,
She tells us that the real world disappears.
Not quite the Donne thing, when push comes to shove:

He wrote betrayal into her delight.
We have a better reason to deceive
Ourselves as we help her help us believe
Life isn't like that: at least, not tonight.

12

It Depends What You Mean by Nonsense

It was Groucho Marx's favourite poem, he said, because it was the only one that 'actually means something'. It's probably known and repeated by more English-speakers than almost any other poem, yet we have no idea who wrote it. And it had already been around for more than a century before Shakespeare was born.

The oldest confirmed variant of 'Thirty Days Hath September' is inscribed in neat handwriting at the bottom of a parchment page in a little leather-bound book in the British Library, dating from the early 1400s. The wording is slightly different from the version we know, but it's unmistakably the same poem. September and November are switched around, but that doesn't matter, for either the calendar or the verse. You certainly don't need to be a scholar of Late Middle English to understand what it's saying, though it's probably helpful to know that fifteenth-century scribes often used a 'j' in place of an 'i' when writing Roman numerals.

Thirti dayes hath novembir
April june and septembir.

Of xxviij is but oon

And alle the remenaunt xxx and j

Most poetry, of course, is useless. But 600 years ago, when ordinary people couldn't read and would never own a book in their lives, a little ditty like this was a thoroughly practical way of remembering and passing on important knowledge. This particular poem has survived because it still performs a useful function. (The Italians have a similar verse, starting 'Trenta giorni ha novembre', but the Germans, French and Russians have to make do with the other mnemonic approach, counting off the months across their knuckles.) And there are plenty of other examples of useful, practical poetry in cultures around the world. Among the nomads of the Sahara, for example, the tribal poets have traditionally played an essential life-or-death role, preserving in their poems the vital ancestral memory of where the waterholes are and how to reach them.

For us, though, much of the time, poetry is seen as a luxury, an optional extra, mysterious, inscrutable, often apparently incomprehensible, often impossibly pretentious. We recognise it by a handful of signs – things like rhyme, metre, metaphor, even the shape it makes on the page – that mark it out from ordinary prose. But there are no common, down-to-earth words that describe the tools the poet uses. We can't talk about poetry in detail without using the kind of terms that immediately remind us of *Private Eye*'s Pseuds Corner. There is no alternative vocabulary, so we are forced to talk about alliteration and assonance, rhyme schemes and consonance, personification and enjambement, anaphora and synecdoche, knowing full well that every mention of them pushes the non-academic reader further and further away from the poem.

But the fact is that poetry – or at least the tools and techniques of poetry – can be seen all around us in our everyday lives. We meet them and feel the force of them, whether consciously or not, in adverts, in headlines, in ordinary conversations. Rhyme comes at us from every direction – Plain Jane, Tricky Dicky, the Thriller in Manila, the Beast from the East. No-one thinks 'Aha, that's alliteration at work' when someone talks about the Fab Four, the Caped Crusader, Sin City, the Lady with the Lamp or the People's Princess. Who cares whether a casual mention of 'Hollywood's favourites', or 'the tabloid press', or 'government red tape', is actually an example of metonymy?

These tricks of the trade are not good or bad in themselves. There's nothing especially wonderful about using rhyme or repetition or alliteration or assonance, except for the effect they can have of making the words vivid in the present and persistent in the memory. When the Ancient Mariner says, 'Yea, slimy things did crawl with legs / Upon the slimy sea', Coleridge is using the rhythm of the verse, the repetition of the word 'slimy' and the subtly slippery alliteration of the S's and L's to create an evocative and unforgettable moment, equally powerful in terms of sound and image. It's all about shaping words and ideas so they are impossible to forget. As Clive's editor and fellow poet Don Paterson says, 'Every device and trope, whether rhyme or metre, metaphor or anaphora, or any one of the thousand others, can be said to have a mnemonic function in addition to its structural or musical one.' In other words, poems are built to be remembered.

In the advertising business, of course, memorability trumps everything, and jingling inanity often counts as success. But elements of art do sometimes rise above the commercial fray. By the time we get to that most pithy, poetic and long-lasting of advertising slogans, 'Beanz Meanz Heinz', dreamed up in 1967 by the Young & Rubicam agency's Mo Drake, it seems almost sacrilegious to pick it apart and see how it works. Its triumph, from a technical point of view, is the way it manages to combine assonance (the repeated '-ea-' vowel sound) and consonance (the triple '-nz' sound) in just three syllables. Its appeal comes from its form as a miniature three-line poem, the rhyming of 'Beanz' and 'Meanz' modulating to a perfect resolution in 'Heinz'. There's the inversion of the natural order of things (the original proposition must surely have been 'Heinz means beans') and the chirpy and distinctive use of –z, rather than –s. 'Oh, and one more thing,' the company probably told the ad agency, 'When you're talking about our baked beans, please don't use the word baked, 'cos they're not – they're stewed. And we don't want any trade descriptions problems.'

The main purpose of poetry (like both advertising and political rhetoric) is to get ideas into our heads and make them stay there, using a range of techniques developed over more than a thousand years. *Beowulf*, for example, which probably dates back to the eighth century, sounds like poetry, even to those who know nothing about Old English. There is no rhyme, but the dense alliteration ('Oft Scyld Scefing sceaþena þreatum, / monegum mægþum, meodosetla ofteah') can be heard, line after line, clearly signalling that this is a worked text, made up of language that has been crafted and massaged according to a particular tradition. And though Lewis Carroll's 'Jabberwocky' gives the initial impression of being almost as impenetrable as *Beowulf*, this masterpiece of literary nonsense announces itself straight away as poetry by its highly conventional use of rhyme and metre.

Everybody loves 'Jabberwocky', but familiarity often blinds us to the way Carroll made it work. For example, though it seems packed with nonsense words (and, famously, added new terms like 'chortle' and 'galumphing' to the English lexicon), it is only really the first verse (repeated at the end of the poem) that hurls a volley of unknown vocabulary at the reader. Allowing for the fact that 'gyre', though unfamiliar, was a long-established Late Middle English term, there are ten invented words packed into that four-line opening stanza:

> 'Twas *brillig*, and the *slithy toves*
> Did gyre and *gimble* in the *wabe*:
> All *mimsy* were the *borogoves*,
> And the *mome raths outgrabe*.

That extraordinary verse was written in 1855, more than ten years before the rest of the poem. At the time, Carroll gave it the title 'Stanza of Anglo-Saxon Poetry'. But when he came to compose the rest of his heroic ballad, which Alice discovers, written in mirror-writing, in *Through the Looking-Glass*, he restricted himself to just three or four nonce words per verse. There are whole lines – 'The jaws that bite, the claws that catch!', 'And stood awhile in thought' – that use ordinary, straightforward Victorian English.

IT DEPENDS WHAT YOU MEAN BY NONSENSE

In fact, you could say that Carroll's 'Jabberwocky' is not nonsense verse at all, but just simple, no-nonsense verse that uses some nonsense vocabulary. The framework laid down by his use of syntax, metre and rhyme is so reassuring that we recognise it immediately as English poetry, even though it introduces twenty-five expressions that simply don't exist in our language.

'Vorpal'? That's OK. It's an adjective. Whatever. We'll come back and work out what it means later. 'Uffish'? Yeah. I get thoughts like that myself, when I'm waiting for monsters to appear. 'Frabjous'? Sounds pretty positive, pretty fabulously gorgeous and fantastic. I've got a general sense of what it's saying. It's no coincidence that 'Jabberwocky' is easy to memorise, despite its apparent strangeness. Alice herself sums it up after reading the text, in a line that could be applied to many lesser poems whose perpetrators would hate them to be seen as nonsense verse. 'It seems very pretty,' she says. 'Somehow it seems to fill my head with ideas – only I don't exactly know what they are!'

Clive has never set out to write nonsense verse as such. But one of his best-known poems, certainly among the tweeters and sharers of the internet generation, is 'Windows Is Shutting Down' – and that has more than a whiff of nonsense about it. It dates from 2005, when Clive was becoming increasingly fed up with what he saw as a depressing and accelerating decline in standards of English grammar and usage. The world was moving online and struggling papers and magazines were starting to cut costs by getting rid of the traditional role of sub-editor, apparently in the belief that Microsoft's spellcheck program could do the same job without demanding a desk or holiday pay. Clive followed up the poem with an outraged and impassioned essay about the problem, under the title 'The Continuing Insult to the Language', in one of his favourite Australian magazines, *The Monthly*, in mid-2006. This cited many examples of hopelessly malformed and ungrammatical sentences from respected writers (including AA Gill) who should have known better. There was no mistaking the anger and frustration that lay behind this 2700-word tirade. But 'Windows Is Shutting Down', ostensibly about the same subject, is a far subtler response to it.

For a start, it's funny. Indeed, to judge by the comments about it that are to be found online, many people see it as purely an amusing exercise in grammatical perversity and enjoy it on that level.

It's true that there is a grim humour about lines like 'A sentence have to be screwed pretty bad / Before they gets to where you doesnt knows / The meaning what it must of meant to had.' But this string of Grand Guignol grammatical car-crashes would never have occurred in real life. Nobody, educated or not, writes, or talks, like that. And the title and first line, 'Windows is shutting down', is neither perverse nor wrong, despite the momentary impression it gives of matching a plural noun with a singular verb. It's no more incorrect than 'Politics is the art of the possible' or 'The Netherlands has many windmills'. So what is Clive actually up to here? Or is he just playing around with the comic possibilities that arise from relentlessly mixing up singulars and plurals (and demonstrating an early awareness of the clickbait potential of writing a poem with this familiar phrase as its title)?

The poem came before Clive's rant in *The Monthly*, and I like to think it may have had a slightly different idea behind it. Although he clearly hates the thought of his beloved English degenerating into an amorphous linguistic slurry, the reference to a mutant language rising from the dead can ultimately be seen as optimistic. He's right that sentences 'have to be screwed pretty bad' before they lose the ability to communicate. Precision may be lost, or temporarily mislaid while new forms develop, but people will still feel the urge to convey meaning. And our language is remarkably resilient. Never mind mashed-up grammar, even jumbled words can be read unexpectedly easily (pdrovied the fsrit and lsat ltetres of a wrod are ccreort, yuor biran wlil siltl regiconse and usatdnernd it wtih spungririsly ltitle dfflicutiy).

It is probably worth remembering that Clive wrote both the poem and the essay that followed in the middle of a period of wild panic about the death of writing. For a few years, everyone assumed that a royal flush of emerging technologies – mobile phones, voice recognition, ebooks, Skype and social networks – would virtually eliminate the need to write, rather than talk, and probably kill off the printed book, too.

What has actually happened, though, is that more people are writing more words now than ever before. There's a lot of recent research that shows that Millennials and the Gen Z kids actually prefer to text, rather than speak on the phone. Their texts and tweets and posts are mostly short, conversational, informal and spontaneous, and the niceties of grammar and punctuation may not be seen as very important when you're tapping something out on the train to work. But we all find ourselves handling many more business and family matters these days by email, rather than by phone. When this happens, the permanence of the written note imposes a need to make our points clearly and with enough grammatical discipline to at least avoid any ambiguity. In response to this, teaching in primary schools has recently acquired a new emphasis on SPaG – spelling, punctuation and grammar – that's surely well-intentioned, though it's also laughably crude, simplistic and prescriptive. (If you think drilling nine-year-olds to recognise and use semi-colons and 'fronted adverbials' is the key to teaching them good writing, you are probably Michael Gove, and I feel sorry for you.) The post-2014 National Curriculum enshrines this misguided pedantry, requiring primary school children to learn forty different grammatical terms (including 'determiners', 'connectives' and 'embedded relative clauses') in the vain hope that this will help them learn to write properly. A few minutes spent poring over the details should be enough to convince anyone that this can't be the best approach to raising standards and protecting English from the perceived drift towards grammatical entropy. But, in the absence of anything more inspired, perhaps our best hope is the spontaneous emergence of the mutant language Clive imagines in 'Windows Is Shutting Down'. If people need to write to communicate, they will find ways to get the message across. If children read and listen (to radio, television or the teachers and other adults around them), they will naturally develop some sense of the shapes and forms that can help them convey information and feelings effectively.

Maybe the poem is right. Maybe 'all them rules is suddenly old hat'. But my guess is that what we'll end up with will not be all that different from the kind of Standard English that has evolved over the centuries – a dynamic, flexible, resilient language, tugged backwards and forwards by the influences of fashion and social change, slang and technology, but still recognisably our mother tongue. After all, if 'Thirty Days Hath September' still makes sense after six hundred years, we're probably not reaching the end of the line just yet.

Windows Is Shutting Down

Windows is shutting down, and grammar are
On their last leg. So what am we to do?
A letter of complaint go just so far,
Proving the only one in step are you.

Better, perhaps, to simply let it goes.
A sentence have to be screwed pretty bad
Before they gets to where you doesnt knows
The meaning what it must of meant to had.

The meteor have hit. Extinction spread,
But evolution do not stop for that.
A mutant languages rise from the dead
And all them rules is suddenly old hat.

Too bad for we, us what has had so long
The best seat from the only game in town.
But there it am, and whom can say its wrong?
Those are the break. Windows is shutting down.

13

That Old Black Magic

When Peter Stothard, editor of the *Times Literary Supplement* from 2002 to 2016, was asked, halfway through his tenure, to name three personal favourites from the hundreds of poems he had published in the magazine, he ducked the question.

He didn't like the idea of picking favourites, and he was even less fond of the notion that poems could be ranked in order, like the winning marrows in the village horticultural show. 'I froze,' he remembers. 'Listophobia again.'

Stothard, a serious Oxford classicist and literary and political journalist who edited *The Times* for ten years before moving on to the *TLS*, is the sort of man who can usually be relied on to put up a stout defence against the trivialities and Top Tens of today's emoji culture. But when he was pressed a second time to choose his favourite *TLS* poems, the temptation was too much. And the poem he put at the very top of his list was 'The Magic Wheel', by Clive James, first published in the *TLS* Christmas issue in 2004.

Compared with the poems of Clive's that had attracted most attention up to that time, it was scarcely an obvious crowdpleaser. It didn't have the inspired cattiness of 'The Book of My Enemy

Has Been Remaindered'. It didn't call attention to itself or court controversy by name-dropping or playing games with the icons of twentieth-century popular culture, like 'Bring Me the Sweat of Gabriela Sabatini', 'Johnny Weissmuller Dead in Acapulco' or his early mock-heroic epic *Peregrine Prykke's Pilgrimage Through the London Literary World*. Instead, it announced itself, somewhat bleakly, as 'An ode in the manner of Theocritus', not necessarily a line to set the pulse racing, unless you happen to be a student of early Greek bucolic poetry.

The reference is to Theocritus's 'Idyll 2', written around 270 BC. In this lengthy poem, the narrator, Simaetha, who has loved and lost, uses all the arts and technology available to her to weave a powerful magic. She burns offerings of barley, bay leaves and bran and a scrap of cloth from her lover's cloak, melts a wax voodoo doll, prays to the moon and casts a dramatic spell, with the help of a traditional magic wheel (the *iunx* or wryneck wheel), that must either bring him back or end his life. The man, Delphis, has deserted her, leaving her desolate and ruined ('He burns my being up, who left me here / No wife, no maiden, in my misery'), and she is determined that if she can't have him, no-one else will.

Simaetha's story is largely forgotten now, though her name lives on among biologists, who have recently adopted it as the scientific name for a whole family of tiny, brightly coloured Australian jumping spiders. The wryneck that gives the magic wheel its name is with us, too. It's a bird like a small woodpecker, with a short beak and the odd habit, when threatened, of stretching its neck to three times its normal length, spinning its head round 180°, hissing loudly and giving an unexpectedly convincing imitation of a snake. Perhaps because of this strangely transformative behaviour, the bird was always associated with witchcraft – early legends told of the goddess Aphrodite tying a wryneck to her four-spoked bronze wheel as she turned it and cast her spells.

Simaetha's repeated incantation, 'O magic wheel, draw hither to my house the man I love', is echoed again and again in Clive's poem. But here the roles are reversed. It is the man who is harking back to what has been lost, dreaming hopelessly that the woman he once loved still wants him and still dreams of the spell that will bring him back or kill him. But, of course, she doesn't. Six years have passed and she's moved on. She has a husband now ('a great dancer' with, the poet is forced to admit, 'kindly eyes') and, what is worse, a son. When he meets the whole family and later strolls with them through the streets of Malta, his dream is over and the illusions end in acceptance: 'I walked the shining streets and all was right and nothing wrong / As the joy of our first moment lived again.'

For Peter Stothard, Clive's inversion of the ancient theme struck a modern, relevant chord, appealing to him because of its classical background, but still achieving something rare and poignant.

'It was a version of a classic – but an unusual, genuinely unforgettable one,' Stothard wrote in his *TLS* blog.

The blog entry bore the headline 'Classic Clive James', but this poem is not classic Clive. Even when they refer to classical themes or historical events, most of his poems do not depend for their effect on a detailed knowledge of these background references. 'The Magic Wheel' does, at least in part. For the reader, like Stothard, who knows and loves the original idyll, the Greek tale runs like a countermelody behind Clive's lines, providing illumination and contrasts that enrich the poem.

In Theocritus, for example, it is Simaetha who has made the running at the start of the affair. She has seen Delphis in the street, decided she likes the cut of his jib and set out to get him, eventually sending her maidservant, Thestylis, to persuade him to visit her. When he comes, she experiences agonies of lust, breaking out in a cold sweat, taking his hand and pulling him down 'onto my soft bed'. Though Delphis apparently mumbles a few words to the effect that he had just been on the point of inviting himself to come to see her anyway, it is clear who is taking the lead in their first erotic encounter. As Simaetha describes it,

> Quickly flesh grew warm against flesh, and our faces
> Became flushed with heat. We whispered sweet nothings.
> There is no need to prolong the tale, dear Moon:
> We went to the very end, and both fulfilled our desires.

In the setting of modern-day Malta, the narrator dreams of his ex-lover dreaming and scheming to get him back. But this is an obvious projection of his own desire. He's the one who's saying, 'I am alone, but with you till I die.' She is getting on with her life, while he sits in his hotel room thinking about magic wheels, spells to reignite a lost love and, possibly, even vengeance.

As the poem progresses, though, reality reasserts itself. In the evening, as they dance in the open air café, the man is still transfixed by her beauty and the way she moves. But the turning point arrives with the first intimation of ordinary domesticity, when she waves an innocent welcome to him from a high window as he labours up the steps and he is met, at the open door, by the settled family unit – father, mother and son. Suddenly he knows she dreams of him no more.

Back in his hotel room, the languidly turning fan, a visual echo of Simaetha's magic wheel, rearranges the air, rather than cooling it, and prompts a new perspective. It stirs the heat slowly, lazily, 'As if it were the gradual work of time, / Which leaves things as they are but changes us and picks the hour / To make us see resentment is a crime'. His fevered longings and discontent are symptoms of an egotistical nostalgia, a sentimental affectation that must be put aside. 'A loving memory forgets', partly because it's the right thing to do, but mainly because the alternative will eat him up and make it impossible to continue any sort of relationship with the woman he used to love.

The proof that he has stopped spinning his magic wheel comes in the evening. The triumphal rockets 'flowering in the darkness high above the *festa*' set the rain alight. They all stroll together through the damp and shining streets and all is right with the world, as he feels again 'the joy of our first moment'. Unlike his earlier dreams and projections, this is something substantial and sustainable, based on a new sense of realism. The narrator's cherished hope that his continuing desire is mirrored in the woman's dreams is finally laid to rest, with the sobering realisation that it was always a vain fantasy: 'I dreamed of you as dreaming that, and now / I know you never did.'

These feelings mark the beginning of a resolution that is finally achieved in the last stanza of the poem, the last scene of the movie, a day or two later. In the heat of a blazing afternoon, he sweats and the fever breaks. The healing process is complete. Instead of praying that she will dream of being in his arms again, he now asks only that she remembers him 'when I am gone' and feels himself glad for the happiness she has found in her new life.

> For my delight in your contentment proves that in the past
> My love must have been true, as it is yet:
> The magic wheel has turned to show what fades and what holds fast.
> Dream this when I am gone: that he was glad for me at last.

The magic wheel has changed now. It is no longer the *iunx*, the wryneck wheel Simaetha used in presenting her ritual offerings to the gods. (*Iunx*, incidentally, has come right down to us, via the Latin forms *iynx* and *jynx*, as the modern word *jinx*, meaning a curse or hex. Nobody but a classical scholar would spot it as associated with ancient Greek woodpeckers, but the link with witchcraft and magic forces lingers still, twenty-three centuries on.) In this final couplet of Clive's poem, the magic wheel has evolved into a strange hybrid, combining the ideas of the Wheel of Fortune and a nineteenth-century magic lantern to 'show what fades and what holds fast'.

For the small minority of Clive's fans who are aware of his long and distinguished career as a songwriter (in collaboration with composer/guitarist Pete Atkin), this idea of a technological tool to reveal what is real and what is not will ring loud bells. Clive and Pete's most famous song, and the title track of their first album, released in 1970, is 'Beware of the Beautiful Stranger'. This tells the story of a sceptical punter who coughs up a quid in a fairground caravan to a gypsy with the traditional crystal ball – and gets the surprise of his life when he discovers himself plugged in to what amounts to a Skype call to the future, with an endless succession of genuinely beautiful, genuinely strange women lining up, one behind the other, to complicate his affairs. 'For the damned, there is *always* a stranger,' sings Pete Atkin. 'There is always a Beautiful Stranger.'

When I first met him, in the early 1970s, this was what Clive was focused on, though he had already been writing poetry for more than ten years. Several early poems had already demonstrated his remarkable gift for encapsulating ideas and experience in compact and memorable forms. Yet he saw himself as a songwriter then, rather than a poet. As the years went by, with his prolific journalism and critical writings leading him on towards a successful career in television, the poetry tended to take a back seat, at least in public. He never stopped writing verse, or song lyrics, but the face we saw on screen – the tiny eyes like 10pt hyphens, the beetling brows and the fixed smirk – became the Clive James everyone thought they knew. ('Fixed smirk' is actually his own phrase, from the poem 'Photo File' – a reminder that few other writers have had either the will or the weaponry to skewer their own faults with Clive's merciless precision.)

When he walked away from television, at the turn of the millennium, poetry quickly resumed its place as one of his major activities. *The Book of My Enemy: Collected Verse 1958-2003* brought together 350 pages of poems, plus a selection of more than fifty song lyrics, a body of work that made it clear to those who had not been paying attention that he had already been a committed, practising poet for more than forty years.

Many of the poems were light comic or satirical verses, but many were serious and ambitious creations, written in a wide variety of styles, rhymed and unrhymed, and covering a vast range of different subjects. If some of the poems seemed to take themselves too seriously, others rejoiced in latching on to subjects never before touched by the wand of poetry. 'Reflections on a Cardboard Box', for example, took the name of a weevil-killing pesticide, Hostathion, and imagined it to be that of a Homeric warrior, fighting alongside Achilles amidst the 'forests of swords' on the plain before Troy. (Clive pulled off a similar trick more recently, and more successfully, in one of the poems in *Injury Time*, in which he characterised Ibrutinib, the most important of his anti-leukaemia chemo pills, as a Marvel Comic hero, grappling hand-to-hand with the hordes of cancer cells surging through his body.)

What few of Clive's short poems over the years have done, though, is tell a straightforward, linear story. 'The Magic Wheel' stands out, in that respect. Clive's poems often contain cross-references to historical events or mythical adventures, and there are several examples of his fondness for abrupt, highly cinematic smash-cuts between different settings and different eras within a single impressionistic poem. But this is different. This time he is laying out his tale in a much more traditional way, as a succession of scenes and events that's vividly imagined and depicted in chronological order as the story unfurls.

Though it may seem oddly anachronistic to think of a love story written in the third century BC as 'cinematic', the original poem by Theocritus is clearly made up of a series of recognisable scenes and sequences that could easily be filmed. But just over a hundred years of cinema have taught us that the fundamentals of the art of storytelling never change. Colour, action, tensions and passion bring stories to life, as they always have done. Character draws us in and makes us care. Conflict ups the stakes, and ambivalence makes us recognise our own uncertainties in other people's predicaments. (Does Simaetha want Delphis back or dead? Does the narrator in 'The Magic Wheel' want his former lover to rekindle their affair or to be happy? Does he care enough about her to place her happiness above his own?) The chemistry that makes a tale speak directly to us is just the same now – in films, novels and narrative poems like this – as it was when Theocritus of Syracuse sat down to write about Simaetha and her efforts to bring her lover back.

Both poems are, of course, fictional stories. Theocritus is not Simaetha. Less obviously, especially in view of the personal and autobiographical nature of most of his more recent poetry, the narrator of 'The Magic Wheel' should not necessarily be identified with Clive James. To see the poem as autobiographical is like assuming that *David Copperfield* will tell us about incidents in the life of Charles Dickens. These are works of the imagination and need to be seen as such.

There are few readers, these days, with Peter Stothard's classical training and easy familiarity with the literature of the Ancient Greeks. But Clive's poem is complete in itself, a powerful and self-contained exploration of an emotional crisis and its resolution. The elements it shares with the original – self-dramatisation, self-justification and a sentimentalised view of straightforward physical lust – are implicit in the English poem, without the need for support from the Greek text. The narrator, like Simaetha, hardly emerges as a heroic figure. Yet there is something engagingly fallible about both protagonists. We might like to feel that we would do better in such situations, but that is probably no more than a testament to our own perennial and almost limitless capacity for self-delusion.

The Magic Wheel
An ode in the manner of Theocritus

O magic wheel, draw hither to my house the man I love.
I dreamed of you as dreaming that, and now
The boxed-in balcony of my hotel room high above
Grand Harbour is a sauna. See the prow
Of that small boat cut silk. Out in the sea
No waves, and there below not even ripples turning light
To glitter: just a glow spread evenly
On flawless water spills into the skyline that last night
Was a jewelled silhouette from right to left and left to right.

Behold, the sea is silent, and silent are the winds.
The not yet risen sun edges the sky
With petal-juice of the Homeric rose as day begins.
I am alone, but with you till I die,

Now we have met again after six years.

Last night we danced on limestone in the open-air café.

I saw one woman sitting there near tears,

Aware that she would never look like you or dance that way –

A blessing, like the blessings that have brought you home to stay.

O magic wheel, draw hither to my house the man I love.

I dreamed of you as dreaming that, until

I saw you wave in welcome from your window high above,

And up the slick hard steps designed to kill,

Like all Valletta staircases bar none,

I went, as if I still had strength, to find your open door

And you, and your tremendous little son,

And your husband, the great dancer, whom I had not met before,

And I met his kindly eyes and knew you dreamed of me no more.

Behold, the sea is silent, and silent are the winds.

Stirred by the ceiling fan, the heat of noon

Refuses to grow cooler as it very slowly spins,

But I take its rearrangement as a boon,

As if it were the gradual work of time,

Which leaves things as they are but changes us and picks the hour

To make us see resentment is a crime.

A loving memory forgets and true regret yields power:

Trust in the long slow aqueduct and not the water tower.

O magic wheel, draw hither to my house the man I love.

I dreamed of you as dreaming that. Tonight

My dream was gone, but flowering in the darkness high above

The *festa*, rockets set the rain alight,

The soft, sweet rain. With you and your young men,

I walked the shining streets and all was right and nothing wrong

As the joy of our first moment lived again.

In the ruins of the opera house a lizard one inch long

Is the small but vibrant echo of an interrupted song.

Bethink thee of my love and whence it comes, O holy Moon.

I dreamed of you as dreaming that, and now

I know you never did. Another day: the afternoon

Burns white as only here the sun knows how,

But a fever is broken when I sweat –

For my delight in your contentment proves that in the past

My love must have been true, as it is yet:

The magic wheel has turned to show what fades and what holds fast.

Dream this when I am gone: that he was glad for me at last.

14

Asma Unpacks Her Pretty Clothes

In 2010, *Vogue* magazine sent one of its most experienced feature writers, Joan Juliet Buck, to Syria to interview the president's wife, the glamorous, British-born former investment banker who had married Bashar al-Assad.

Asma, a Sunni Muslim who had grown up in a pebble-dashed house in Acton, West London, and attended the local Twyford Church of England High School, was known to her school chums as Emma. She was bright, slim, smiling, modern and articulate. She had studied at King's College London and emerged with a first class degree in computer science before going to work for Deutsche Bank and JPMorgan. When she married Bashar, the shy, lisping ophthalmologist who had become president a few months before, on the death of his tyrannical father, Hafez al-Assad, she became a symbol of hope and optimism for the future of Syria. It was 2000. She was twenty-five. She wore jeans and sweaters, as well as impeccably understated Chanel suits, and the world expected great things of her.

Asma's energy, youth and charisma were plain for all to see. And the initial signs were good. She quickly became involved in a range of reform programmes and charitable activities concerned with rural microfinance, women's rights, child cancer and disabilities. The United Nations got behind her initiatives and set up an $18 million UN Development Programme to help fund a number of reform projects.

In the years that followed, Asma was the acceptable face of Bashar's authoritarian regime. The Assads rubbed shoulders with a wide range of Western opinion-formers, from David Miliband, John Kerry and Nicolas Sarkozy to Sting and his wife, Trudie Styler. *Paris Match* called Asma 'the element of light in a country full of shadow zones'. 'Sexy Brit bringing Syria in from the cold' panted the *Sun*. In 2008, the Italians awarded her the President's Gold Medal for her humanitarian efforts. In 2009, Angelina Jolie – a committed and tireless Goodwill Ambassador for the UN High Commissioner for Refugees since 2001 – visited Syria for the second time in three years, along with Brad Pitt, and had dinner with the Assads. The visit was intended to focus attention on the UNHCR's work with Iraqi refugees in Syria, but it was bound to provide favourable publicity around the world for Asma and her increasingly insecure and ruthless husband.

The West's insistent desire to see Asma as some kind of cross between Mother Teresa, Marilyn Monroe, Eleanor Roosevelt and Princess Diana continued unabated. So when *Vogue* was offered the unique opportunity to send a journalist to spend time with Syria's First Lady, in late 2010, it was just Joan Juliet Buck's bad luck to be chosen to make the trip and write the profile of this enticingly enigmatic woman.

The *Vogue* article, complete with moody photography and the wince-inducing headline 'A Rose in the Desert', was published in

February 2011. Its flattering tone – the result of Joan Juliet Buck's inevitable compromises, both in Syria and in the writing-up process, and the magazine's insistence that it should be a personality profile without a hint of political insight – caused a storm of protest. But it wasn't the writer's fault. The world had changed. The *Vogue* feature had been overtaken by the march of history. On the very day that Buck had been treated to a homemade fondue in the kitchen of the Assads' apartment, the Arab Spring had begun, with the first disturbances in Tunisia, sparked by the death of a twenty-six-year-old street vendor who had set himself on fire in protest at persecution by the authorities. Demonstrations quickly followed in Algeria, Jordan, Oman, Egypt and Yemen and spread across the Middle East. By the time Joan Juliet Buck's piece was printed, Egypt's Hosni Mubarak, president for the last thirty years, was on the brink of resigning, after eighteen days of sit-ins, speeches and violent clashes in Tahrir Square.

In Syria itself, a small protest about police brutality on 26 January 2011 was followed by 'Day of Rage' demonstrations in Damascus in early February. As tensions grew over the next few weeks, police in Daraa, near the Jordanian border, arrested and tortured fifteen boys, some as young as nine years old, for spraying anti-government graffiti on the walls of their school. Parents and neighbours began daily protests, which spread to Damascus, Aleppo and other cities, and the police and security forces responded with calculated savagery. The Assad empire had begun the descent into all-out civil war.

For Joan Juliet Buck, the very idea of interviewing Asma al-Assad for *Vogue* had initially been a non-starter.

'Send a political journalist,' she had said. 'I don't want to meet the Assads, and they don't want to meet a Jew.'

She was sure she was only being asked because others had turned the job down or been rejected by the Syrians. When she eventually allowed herself to be persuaded, the assignment turned into a bigger personal and professional disaster than she could ever have imagined.

'Syria gave off a toxic aura,' she wrote afterwards. 'But what was the worst that could happen? I would write a piece for *Vogue* that missed the deeper truth about its subject. There was no way of knowing, as I cheered the events in Tahrir Square, that I would be contaminated because I had written about the Assads. There was no way of knowing this piece would cost me my livelihood and end the association I had had with *Vogue* since I was twenty-three.'

Buck was then sixty-two. She had worked for *Vogue* in London, Paris (seven successful years as editor-in-chief of the magazine's French edition) and New York. Her assignment had been no picnic. Her laptop was rifled and her Syrian phone was undoubtedly bugged. She was spied on at every turn and sharply rebuked when she dared to have a brief conversation with the French ambassador. Worse was to come, though, when she got back home. After insisting on four rewrites, each blander than the last, *Vogue* was happy to accept and publish her carefully constructed 3000-word feature. But when things suddenly turned nasty and the furore over the 'Rose in the Desert' profile became too embarrassing, the magazine made Joan Juliet Buck the scapegoat and declined to renew her contract, effectively ending her journalistic career.

Like everyone else, Clive had been seduced by the mirage – the blithely hopeful assumption that Asma, this cool, educated and impossibly stylish woman, would somehow bring an end to the Assad family's hereditary kleptocracy. Sitting in the sunlit, book-lined study of his little house in Cambridge, after years of war and half a million deaths in Syria, he regrets his eagerness to buy into her myth-building. But he is proud of the poem that grew out of his disillusionment.

'When I wrote "Asma Unpacks Her Pretty Clothes", I was trying to face up to my own disappointment and the fact that I had been duped by her image,' he says. 'Asma had impressed me, and the burden of the poem is that it's hard to think straight about a beautiful woman in lovely clothes. It's a very simple reaction. If you're going to search the world for a man who's going to forgive, in advance, a fascist dictator's wife who happens to be wearing gorgeous clothes, I'm the one. It's based on my weakness, not hers.'

The poem is terse and self-contained. It refers directly to Joan Juliet Buck's article ('I doted, as *Vogue* did, on her sheer style') and demands no prior knowledge of the situation in Damascus. In thirty lines, it evokes the sensuous, self-involved decadence of Asma's privileged lifestyle ('With her perfect hands, she helps' as her ladies unpeel the silk and cashmere from the 'clinging leaves of tissue') and contrasts this tactile luxury with the sadistic brutality of the torturers' routines.

It doesn't spell out the detail of Asma's £4000 diamond-encrusted Christian Louboutin shoes and her Parisian crystal chandeliers, because it doesn't need to. Though she has always spent lavishly, like any top-drawer dictator's wife, her personal style has always been, as the *Vogue* piece pointed out, 'not the couture-and-bling dazzle of Middle Eastern power but a deliberate lack of adornment'. 'Cunning understatement', Joan Juliet Buck called it, in one of the subtly subversive comments that hinted at Asma's manipulative skills and made the *Vogue* profile rather less of a fawning tribute than her critics would allow. (Buck had also, for example, drawn attention to the First Lady's breathlessly girlish speech patterns – 'I was, like, "Please, I just want to get out" and he was "Don't worry, it happens to the best of us"' – and pointedly referred to Bashar's 'startling 97 per cent of the vote' when he was elected president.)

For years, people in the West sought to explain how Asma's supposedly benign influence had failed to stop the tragedy in Syria. She was a prisoner, they said, trapped in the eye of the storm and forced, by her husband or by the powers behind the throne, to do and say just what suited their purposes. Her public appearances were rare and obviously stage managed. Perhaps she was permanently drugged. Or she was not in Syria at all. She'd been spirited away to exile in Russia or any one of a dozen other countries. But the *Vogue* profile, for all its limitations, argued strongly against any of those later interpretations. The woman Joan Juliet Buck met was healthy, self-confident, relaxed, energetic and clearly convinced of her own righteousness. In those last days before the war started, she was enjoying life. She spoke and acted like a wife with a warm and uncritical relationship with her murderous spouse, and a rare media appearance, on Russian TV six years later, confirmed her continued insistence that Syria's agony is not his fault. In December 2018, Asma, now forty-three, was photographed, hairless and headscarved, after being treated in a military hospital in Damascus for breast cancer, though she continued to make visits to children's hospitals, women's groups and wounded soldiers. In August 2019, it was announced that she had made a full recovery. 'My journey is over,' she told Syrian state TV. 'I totally conquered cancer.'

For people who have known Clive James only as a playfully witty journalist, critic, memoirist and television personality, or, more recently, as a poet mainly concerned with highly personal issues of death and dying, the political nature of this short poem may come as a surprise. For those who have read the serious, passionate and panoramically well-informed historical and biographical essays that make up his prose masterwork, *Cultural Amnesia*, there will be no such surprise. But Clive is always at his best when he finds his own individual way into a subject. Years ago, wearing his other hat as a lyricist, he wrote a wonderful song about the children of Auschwitz, 'A Hill of Little Shoes'. What set that apart from any other account of the horrors of the death camps was the abrupt realisation that he and the children who died were exact contemporaries. Clive had been born in 1939. As the song points out, if he had been in Europe, rather than Australia, he might have shared their fate.

They were like you in the same year.
But you grew up.
They were scarcely even here,
Before they suddenly weren't there.

As he says, he 'was chosen to grow old', while hundreds of thousands of children of his age were chosen by the industrialised killing machine of Nazi Germany for immediate extinction.

In 'Asma Unpacks Her Pretty Clothes', Clive once more takes it very personally indeed. It's not just that he shares the general disappointment and dashing of expectations. He feels personally guilty for having fallen under Asma's spell, for having been caught up in a romanticised, quasi-erotic seduction that revolved around his own 'weakness', rather than her actual potential to change Syria's destiny. It's the no-fool-like-an-old-fool syndrome, coupled with Clive's lifelong susceptibility to the magnetism of a pretty face. When he writes 'So now my blood is curdled by the shrieks / Of people mad with grief. My own wrists hurt', it is a visceral, physical reaction to the shame he feels at having been taken in by Asma's deadly charm and having been, in his own small, vicarious way, complicit in what has occurred under Assad's iron fist.

Clive is pleased with the way the poem has retained its power and relevance. The blank verse form – unrhymed iambic pentameters – suits the subject, accommodating colloquial speech patterns ('We sort of knew, but he had seemed so modern') within the discipline of a measured and formal structure. The phrasing is spare and direct, largely undecorated, with few adjectives and just one understated instance of self-conscious wordplay ('the Middle Ages / Brought back to living death'). And, though the tone is almost that of documentary reportage, jump-cutting between the hushed serenity of Asma's residence and the grim horror of the torturers' cells, the amount of background detail that's included seems finely judged. It is, in visual terms, a tightly edited poem.

'The trap, when you're writing about anything with a political dimension, is that you become over-explanatory,' says Clive. 'And the other trap, of course, is that you are so aware of this danger that you err in the opposite direction. If, as you say, it seems sure-footed in its choices about what to include and what to leave out, I take that as a very real compliment. It's an important poem for me, and I'd like it to last.'

Asma Unpacks Her Pretty Clothes

Wherever her main residence is now,
Asma unpacks her pretty clothes.
It takes forever: so much silk and cashmere
To be unpeeled from clinging leaves of tissue
By her ladies. With her perfect hands, she helps.

Out there in Syria, the torturers
Arrive by bus at every change of shift
While victims dangle from their cracking wrists.
Beaten with iron bars, young people pray
To die soon. This is the Middle Ages
Brought back to living death. Her husband's doing,
The screams will never reach her where she is.

Asma's uncovered hair had promised progress
For all her nation's women. They believed her.

We who looked on believed the promise too,
But now, as she unpacks her pretty clothes,
The dream at home dissolves in agony.

Bashar, her husband, does as he sees fit
To cripple every enemy with pain.
We sort of knew, but he had seemed so modern
With Asma alongside him. His big talk
About destroying Israel: standard stuff.
A culture-changing wife offset all that.

She did, she did. I doted as *Vogue* did
On her sheer style. Dear God, it fooled me too,
So now my blood is curdled by the shrieks
Of people mad with grief. My own wrists hurt

As Asma, with her lustrous fingertips –
She must have thought such things could never happen –
Unpacks her pretty clothes.

15

The Editor's Blue Pencil

Poetry is personal. Almost by definition, it is packed and compact, finding meaning in the collision of form and content, setting its own terms of reference, making demands on the reader and going where its author chooses to go. Often, as we all know, it ends up going haywire and failing both writer and reader. But idiom and idiosyncrasy are part of what we expect. So where does the idea of editing someone else's poetry fit in?

We'd be surprised to hear that a colleague had invaded the painter's studio, grabbing a brush and relocating a Cubist eye, adding a sunflower, brightening up a Rothko or tidying up a Jackson Pollock. We'd expect a Beethoven or a Fauré to turn a deaf ear to any outsider's ideas about improving a symphony or jazzing up a D minor requiem by shifting it into B flat. But we all know that books are edited, even great books by great writers. One particularly influential New York editor, Maxwell Perkins, described by his biographer as 'editor, manager, moneylender, psychoanalyst and father confessor' to his authors, is credited with reshaping the twentieth-century American novel in the course of his long working relationships with Hemingway, F Scott Fitzgerald and many others.

Max Perkins would propose, cajole, amend and encourage. But, above all, he would cut. Cutting back superfluous words, phrases, sentences, paragraphs, pages, anecdotes and chapters was his greatest skill. Paring the text down to its essentials, he would help his authors bring out the best in their material. Like the *diamantaires* of Antwerp, who have known for centuries that 50 per cent of every rough diamond must be lost in the process of cleaving, faceting and polishing to release the inner fire and produce the finest gemstones, he understood that, in prose, less is almost always more. But that's prose. The very idea of editing and amending a poet's work seems almost blasphemous.

We're used to the idea that poetry editors are curators, compiling anthologies and helping individual poets decide what should be included in their slim volumes, what the running order should be and how it should be presented. What we're not so familiar with is the actual engagement with the text of a poem. Yet this is a necessary process that has been going on for centuries.

Back in 1800, William Wordsworth used to send his poems off to the brilliant scientist and earnestly dreadful amateur poet, Humphry Davy, for him to proofread them and make any corrections he saw fit. Wordsworth was a poetic revolutionary in many ways (including effectively reviving the English sonnet after a break of more than a century), but he was surprisingly offhand about this aspect of his work. Davy was an interesting choice as an editor – a true pioneer of modern chemistry, addicted to laughing gas and later, famously, the inventor of the miner's safety lamp. But Wordsworth did not meet him till much later, and Davy's unpaid work on the *Lyrical Ballads* was sloppy and inconsistent, a fact that did not seem to bother the high-minded Romantic.

In the years after the First World War, TS Eliot had Ezra Pound looking over his shoulder as he worked on the draft of *The Waste Land*, chipping in with bold and sometimes quite disparaging remarks. 'Make up yr mind', 'Perhaps be damned', 'Too loose' and 'Verse not interesting enough as verse to warrant so much of it' he commented.

'Too tum-pum at a stretch' Pound wrote, when he read 'A Game of Chess', the second part of Eliot's masterpiece. When Eliot lapsed into an over-predictable iambic pentameter rhythm, Pound chided him ('Too penty') and bullied him into rewriting until he earned an approving 'OK' in the margin. Even *The Waste Land*'s sonorous introduction, 'April is the cruellest month', only emerged as its opening gambit after Pound had read through and rejected a lengthy fifty-four-line preamble recounting a night out on the razzle in downtown Boston.

That oddly productive editorial relationship is commemorated in one of Clive's early poems, 'Simple Stanzas about Modern Masters'. 'One had the gab, the other had the gift,' he wrote. 'And each looked to the other for a lift.' Politically, Pound was poison, but his cultural influence, in the years before he spiralled into antisemitism and starry-eyed adulation of Mussolini and Hitler, was immense. This is Clive in playful light verse mode, sounding a bit like Ogden Nash, but the point is well made.

The Waste Land, had not Pound applied his blue
Pencil, might well have seemed less spanking new.

Pound was a crackpot but that made his critical
Prowess particularly analytical.

In his 'Letter to a Young Poet', printed as an afterword to the poems in *Injury Time*, Clive spells out the value of having a critical friend, a better self, who can nudge the author towards recognising potential weaknesses in a poem.

'It helps to have a brilliant, sensitive and critically scrupulous friend to read your completed manuscript, but only if his objections are those that you would have made yourself, given time.'

For the young poet, finding the right soulmate and sounding-board may be difficult. But one of the luxuries that comes with being an established and experienced poet is the chance to build a long-term relationship with a professional editor who is on the same wavelength.

So I was interested, early in the preparation of this book, to meet Don Paterson, knowing that he had been Clive's poetry editor at Picador for more than twenty years and was an award-winning, internationally recognised poet in his own right. How did the relationship work? Did the younger man really question and criticise Clive's drafts? If his critical scruples prompted an intervention, would Paterson feel it was his duty to propose deletions and weigh in with amendments and suggestions for rephrasing?

Don Paterson's credentials are impeccable. The other poets on his list at Picador have included the recent poet laureate Carol Ann Duffy, Peter Porter, Michael Donaghy, Kate Tempest and more than thirty other practitioners, though the boot's on the other foot when it comes to his own poetry, which is published (and edited) by Faber & Faber.

'People have this idea that editing poetry is different, that a poem is somehow precious and special and you can't edit it like any other piece of writing,' says Paterson. 'But you can. You just need to understand the rules.'

The key, he says, is to put your ideas and prejudices to one side, focus intensely on the draft text and try to recognise what the poem is trying to do.

'You have to identify what the vision of the poet is and make some reckoning of the shortfall between what you see on the page and what you sense is the direction the work wants to go in.'

Then it's simply a matter of trying to help the author, of going through the text, line by line, and marking the things that could potentially be done better.

'Clive's been a hero of mine since I was thirteen. I would read every bit of his television criticism I could find, and his *Unreliable Memoirs* set the standard, for me, of what a masterly piece of autobiography should look like. So it was hard working with him at first. For the first few years, I kept pinching myself and trying to pretend I was relaxed about the whole thing, but I was too much in awe of him to contribute anything very useful.'

In the end, though, the process began to reassert itself. Paterson, who had left school at sixteen and started life as a jazz guitarist before beginning to write his own poetry and drifting into editing by accident, started to gain the necessary confidence and experience to work alongside Clive and other idols of his youth, such as Peter

Porter. He began to enjoy the role of foil and confidant and feel his suggestions were valued, even if they weren't always accepted.

'Sometimes it's a structural thing, where you've got to lose a couple of stanzas to keep the poem focused,' he says. 'Sometimes it's technical – you're arguing about a point of metre or rhyme or about whether a metaphor is working. Sometimes it's to do with consistency – if the poem is really about two things when it should be about just one.

'With some authors you do more; with others, less. You do less with the authors who know what they're doing. And, believe me, Clive knows exactly what he's doing. He knows I know, so when I do make a suggestion, he knows I've thought about it and he takes it seriously, even if, in the end, he decides not to change a thing.'

Don Paterson sees the whole issue of editing poetry from both sides of the desk. He is the only man to have won the TS Eliot Prize for Poetry twice (alongside other winners who include Ted Hughes, Seamus Heaney, Carol Ann Duffy and Derek Walcott) and his 2009 collection, *Rain*, won the Forward Prize. But his own poetry editor at Faber, Matthew Hollis, is known as a tough and demanding collaborator, impressed, maybe, but not cowed by Paterson's successes.

'Matthew's a fine poet with a miserably accurate eye,' growls Paterson, though he admits the editor delivers his insights with kid gloves and 'always softens the really bad news with extravagant praise'.

Hollis, in turn, as you will already have guessed by now, is published by Bloodaxe, rather than Faber. That's how it goes in the trunk-to-tail elephants' circle of poetry publishing. But Paterson is convinced the fact that many of the UK's most influential poetry editors are also practising poets makes for bold decisions and high standards.

Despite his earlier comments, editing poetry, he admits, is not quite like editing prose. It's about 'tiny shifts of sense and emphasis, context and connection' and the very nature of poetry means that it is likely to be 'fuelled by high emotion, or at least inspirations that are highly personal', making it easy for the author to lose a sense of perspective.

'A non-poet can't do a line-edit on a poem,' says Paterson. 'And I'm a line-editor guy, really. When I'm working with Clive, I just go through what he's written and underline the things I think might be changed, that could maybe be done better. It's never an edict, though, always a conversation.'

So does he really try to correct Clive's metaphors, if he thinks they're not quite working?

'Occasionally. And Clive will correct them back again most of the time, probably quite rightly. But he can be ruthless with his own work. When you sit down with him and suggest – as you always have to do with all Australian poets – that the first stanza should be deleted, he'll do it. He's happy to sacrifice anything, if it makes the poem work better.'

Paterson is used to wearing his two hats – as poet and as editor – and he's comfortable in both. But he finds switching between the different roles surprisingly easy, as he explained in a recent blog interview with poet and novelist Isabel Rogers.

'The amazing thing is the speed with which you can ditch the edit-y hat, the one with the little green visor and the fake ear with the blue pencil behind it, for the author's hat. That's the knitted one with a lopsided pom-pom, of the sort you'd see on a two-year-old, covered in snot and tears and very dirty from being thrown out of the pram a lot. I can get into that one pretty quick.'

What the editor must do, he says, is give the poet the opportunity to get a new perspective by using someone else's eyes, unblinded by any sentimental attachment to the work.

'I keep myself – and the kind of poem I'd write – out of the picture. It has nothing to do with me. Editors shouldn't edit poems into the kind of poems they like. The poets I work with know what they're doing. All I really do is remind them of that.'

One obvious temptation for the editor of Clive James's poetry must be the seductive nature of his verbal skills. In all his different roles – as journalist, critic, essayist, TV front-man, memoir-writer, lyricist and poet – the sheer energy and bravado of his wit and imagery have been his hallmark. This is the man who, way back in 1978, reviewed a feeble BBC classic serial under the crushing headline 'Wuthering Depths'. This is the man whose aphorisms ('It is only when they go wrong that machines remind you how powerful they are', 'Fiction is life with the dull bits left out' and many more) are splattered and misquoted across the Twittersphere. This is the man whose 'Valediction for Philip Larkin' includes the haunting image of giraffes floating across the Kenyan plains 'like anglepoise lamps in zero g', who coins startling, unforgettable phrases to immortalise the trivial, encapsulate the ineffable and dazzle the unwary reader at every turn.

When someone has this extraordinary gift for making words sing and dance and turn somersaults, it must be hard for the editor to get to grips with the substance of a poem. Paterson recognises the problem, and the matchless flair that causes it. But he refuses to be blinded by the light.

'The glittering phrasemaking is there all right, and it's one of the things I admire most about his TV criticism, for example. But the poems are doing something different,' he says.

'The poems aren't quite what you'd expect from Clive. They're not about the cleverness of one great line after another. They're integrated compositions. They're doing something quite unfashionable, which is making an argument – often a moral argument – in the way that Larkin used to do.'

There's a contrast here, Paterson believes, with other poets who are known for their verbal dexterity and conceptual pyrotechnics.

'Look at the work of someone like Craig Raine, for example. Many of Raine's effects, considered individually, are quite astonishing. But you'll often find that they disrupt the whole. Clive's effects don't do that. You don't feel they've been gratuitously shipped in. They contribute. These poems are a whole lot more than the sum of their effects.'

The twenty-year working relationship between Clive and Don Paterson is based on affection, as well as mutual respect. But Clive knows that Don's role, representing the readers who will eventually hold the book in their hands, adds an important element. While any poet, inevitably, sees publication of his or her work at least partly in terms of building a career or establishing a legacy, the editor's perspective is necessarily different.

'The editor's position is a practical one,' Clive wrote in his *Poetry Notebook*. 'He or she is more concerned with printing something attractive to read than with helping to decide starting positions in the world-historical struggle towards immortality. The very best are usually poets themselves, so they have felt all this on the skin.'

Clive's admiration for Paterson's skills and judgement means that he takes the job of editing, revision and reworking very seriously. He's convinced the long hours of discussion and argument add value and he's happy to invest a lot of time and effort in the process.

'He'll sweat you until you get it right,' he says. 'Don's very sharp, very clever. I'm extremely lucky to have him in my corner. He makes me feel like an ageing welterweight with Mike Tyson as my second.'

During one of our interviews in connection with this book, in November 2017, Clive thrust a thick bundle of typescript papers at me across the table. It was the first complete draft of his last long poem, *The River in the Sky*, and he was already working with Paterson to edit it for publication.

'No-one's supposed to be seeing it at this stage,' he grinned. 'I promised myself I wouldn't do this. Don would kill me if he knew I was showing it to you. And it may change a lot. It's on its way, but it may be very different by the time it's published, which will be about a year from now. Don will have his, er, requirements.'

Quite apart from the changes negotiated between Clive and Don Paterson, there were always several other people influencing the way *The River in the Sky* progressed towards its final form. Clive has the advantage of the high-powered collection of trusted friends he calls his 'in-house critics', a group that includes Ian McEwan, Martin Amis, Tom Stoppard and two eminent Australians, novelist and critic David Free and poet Stephen Edgar. Several rough copies of the draft manuscript had already been sent out to these first readers, and the responses were already coming in, including one that seemed to echo Ezra Pound's advice to TS Eliot about removing the first fifty lines or so of the draft of *The Waste Land*.

'Somebody suggested – it was Stoppard, actually – that *The River in the Sky* would be better without the first hundred lines. That's a very common approach from him. He's always thinking about how it would work if he were having to put it on the stage.'

Stoppard also demonstrated an acute eye for factual detail, pulling Clive up sharply and insisting that he should change a line where he had made an elementary mistake about the kind of stuffing used in Jiffy bags.

But it is Don Paterson's uncanny ability to detect unnecessary padding that Clive admires most.

'Don's particularly good at recognising when a poem is over,' he says. 'If you read his book about Shakespeare's sonnets, you'll see he often suggests that Shakespeare would have done better to leave off the final, clinching couplet.'

That kind of unflinching understanding about where to draw the line is an asset Clive has valued for many years. In his poem 'Visitation of the Dove', from *Injury Time*, it resulted in the last-minute amputation of a final stanza that Paterson felt was redundant.

'Visitation of the Dove' was first published, as a four-stanza poem, in *The New Yorker* in December 2015. After the last line of the third verse, 'The dove flies', there was a whole stanza more:

And as it lifts away I start these last
Few lines, for I know that my song must end.
It will be done, and go back to the past,
But I wish still
To be here watching when the leaves descend.
I might yield then, perhaps. But not until.

Paterson took the view that this extra verse weakened the poem and diluted its impact. Clive disagreed, though he was happy to rewrite the lines more than once to try to accommodate his editor's reservations. Paterson stood firm. He was determined that the definitive version of the poem, in the book, should end with the dove's ascent.

'Don is especially good at quietly pulling a sour face,' says Clive. 'And however much I modified the stanza, he went right on pulling it. "It's over when the dove takes off," he said. And finally, of course, I realised he was dead right.'

Visitation of the Dove

Night is at hand already: It is well
That we yield to the night. So Homer sings,
As if there were no Heaven and no Hell,
But only peace.

The grey dove comes down in a storm of wings
Into my garden where seeds never cease

To be supplied as if life fits a plan
Where needs are catered to. One need is not:
I do not wish to leave yet. If I can
I will stay on
And see another autumn, having got
This far with all my strength not yet quite gone.

When Phèdre, dying, says that she can see
Already not much more than through a cloud,
She adds that death has taken clarity
Out of her eyes
To give it to the world. Behold my shroud!
This brilliance in the garden. The dove flies.

16

Diana

The night Princess Diana and her lover, Emad 'Dodi' Al Fayed, were killed in a car crash in Paris, on 31 August 1997, the world was shocked. In Britain and around the globe, there was a huge public outpouring of grief. Nothing so stunningly dramatic has happened in the last two decades or more, except perhaps the Twin Towers tragedy on 11 September 2001. Nothing else has had the same shattering international impact, or seemed so arbitrarily, annihilatingly evil. After Diana's funeral, excitable commentators repeated the dubious claim that two billion people, a third of the world's population, had watched the service on television.

Objectively, of course, Diana's death and the 9/11 catastrophe are not remotely comparable. Three people died in the crash in the Pont de l'Alma tunnel; nearly 3000 were killed in the attack on the World Trade Center, and the geopolitical axis of the world was shifted for ever. But the emotional impact of the two events was similar. Millions were left dazed and appalled by Diana's passing, ambushed by the strength of their feelings and the unexpected sense of personal bereavement. For sixteen years she had been the world's most photographed woman. She had been the fairytale princess, wife of the heir apparent, future queen, mother of the next generation of royal princes. When the strains in her marriage to Prince Charles started to show, leading to a four-year separation and eventual divorce, she became, if anything, even more fascinating, in her new role as the star of a global soap opera.

When she fell in love with Dodi, the playboy son of Mohamed Al Fayed, the former sewing machine salesman who owned Harrods and had recently bought Fulham Football Club, the world's media erupted into an orgy of excitement, Mills & Boon-like myth-making and prurient curiosity.

It is easy to forget, at this distance, that the whole affair lasted just one month. This was never going to be like Abelard and Héloïse, Victoria and Albert, Bogart and Bacall or Paul and Linda. At the time, though, it was the biggest story in town.

Diana was coming to the end of a deep and passionate two-year relationship with Hasnat Khan, a shy, self-effacing Pakistani-born heart surgeon who worked at the Royal Brompton Hospital. In July 1997, she accepted an invitation to get away from it all on Mohamed Al Fayed's $20 million yacht, the *Jonikal*, which was moored off St Tropez. Within two days, Dodi arrived, closely followed by his fiancée, the American model Kelly Fisher, who was wearing a huge diamond and sapphire engagement ring he had bought her. For the next few days, Fisher was parked on a smaller Al Fayed yacht nearby while Dodi and the princess relaxed together, flirted and fell in love. As the eventual inquest into the Paris deaths learned, from the verbatim transcript of a taped twenty-minute phone call, she was not at all happy about this.

'You even flew me down to St Tropez to sit on a boat while you seduced Diana all day and fucked me all night,' she said, while Dodi shouted back that she was 'crazy' and 'hysterical'. By the time the famous paparazzi snapshot of Diana and Dodi kissing on the deck of the *Jonikal* appeared in the *Sunday Mirror*, on 10 August, Kelly Fisher knew she had been written out of the script. She flew home and launched a breach of contract action, which she duly dropped after the crash.

Dodi was always going to be trouble. He made enemies, bounced cheques and ran up debts, renting lavish hotel suites and beachside holiday homes and hiring bodyguards and private planes wherever he went. At the age of forty-two, he struggled to survive on the $100 000-a-month allowance provided by his father and it was claimed that, at one stage, he was in the habit of spending $15 000 a week on cocaine for himself and his entourage. One friend told *Vanity Fair* magazine about the 'cokehead' scene in the Waldorf Towers suite Dodi had rented in New York. 'The only time I ever saw a kilo of cocaine was in Dodi's apartment,' he said.

Others remember him as gentle, generous and fun to be with – 'without guile, though not without bullshit', according to one lifelong friend. Clive didn't know Dodi, but he knew enough about him to know that he wouldn't like him. That wasn't the point, though. Diana was the story, not her lover. And Diana had the knack of bringing out whatever was good in the people she met.

'She had the gift of reflecting a man's best self back to him,' Clive wrote, two years after her death. 'Redeeming features in Dodi Fayed are hard to find, but it is a safe bet that when he was near her he was at his best. She probably saw something in him, and got him to agree.'

Everybody, of course, saw Diana in a different light, whether they knew her as a friend or had only seen her on television or read about her in the tabloid press. To some she was an empty-headed party girl, out of her depth and permanently floundering. To others, she was the bulimic, self-harming depressive, forced into an intolerable and unprecedented situation within the Royal Family and British society. Some saw her as beautiful, kind, energetic, inspiring – the sort of person who could light up a room just by walking into it, who would hug an AIDS victim or a leprosy sufferer, spend hours every week with elderly or homeless people or children with cancer and campaign tirelessly, sometimes in the face of political opposition, against the use of landmines. Others saw her as manipulative, unstable and dangerous to know.

Not many, though, knew her like Clive James did. Over the last few years of her life, he would meet her for quiet, intimate, talkative lunches, first, at her invitation, in the privacy of Kensington Palace, later, at his, at Le Caprice. Once the rhythm was established, they would get together once or twice a year, either at posh and discreet restaurants like Launceston Place, Bibendum or Kensington Place or back at the palace.

'She liked the Caprice when she wanted to hide in public, and Kensington Place and Launceston Place when she was really hiding,' says Clive.

She would pick his brains and laugh at his jokes; he would bask in the intoxicating energy of her presence. They would share secrets and desserts and he would deftly straddle the ambiguity of his roles as friend and adviser to Prince Charles and platonic chevalier to his estranged wife.

When the news of Diana's death came through, Clive was devastated, struck dumb with shock and grief. While every journalist on the planet snapped into action to hammer out the obituaries and think-pieces that would fill the world's papers and magazines, Clive, who had actually known her, sat still and silent at his desk, unwilling to answer the dozens of messages begging him to give the press what it craved. It was his old friend, Tina Brown, then editor of *The New Yorker*, who tempted him out into the open, promising him unlimited space to write whatever he wanted, challenging him to go beyond the stereotyping and talk about the real person and finally asking, 'What the hell else are you going to do for the next few days?'

The response was an anguished, highly personal story that took twenty minutes to read and ninety-six hours to write. It appeared in a special memorial edition of *The New Yorker*, then in the *Sunday Telegraph* and subsequently in various forms, edited, abridged and translated, in hundreds of other publications around the world. More than twenty years on, in the cold light of day, it is still a remarkable piece of writing – colourful and revealing, gossipy and self-indulgent, doting and analytical, comprehensive in its scope and dazzling in its deliberate, self-conscious craftsmanship. Clive knew he was writing for posterity, and he deployed all the skills and artistry he could muster to create a prose poem, 4700 words long, that would honour and illuminate his subject. Some of his technical devices are immediately obvious. Every one of the twenty-three paragraphs begins with the word 'No' – sometimes used to create a sense of conversational continuity ('No, I didn't see her again for a long time'), sometimes to emphasise a negative point ('No life, and no future'). The picture of their relationship is built up, scene by scene, assembled with all the attention to setting, storyline, dialogue and pacing of a Hollywood movie. The penultimate sequence describes Diana leaving Le Caprice by the back door to avoid the photographers. It ends with a flurry of glimpses – 'She's turning her head. She's smiling. Has she forgotten something? Is she coming back?' – that sets up the final, inevitable, monosyllabic paragraph.

'No.'

Later, Clive came right out with it and claimed the status of poetry for this article.

'If you believe, as I do, that a poem is any piece of writing that can't be quoted from except out of context, then a poem is what my lament for the Princess is, at least in the eyes of its author,' he wrote. It's a fine, quotable aphorism, even if, on examination, it adds up to slightly less than meets the eye. The point is that he threw everything he had into this threnody – feelings, observations, jokes, anecdotes and indiscretions – to ensure he gave it his best shot. If it's not quite poetry, it's certainly a highly poetic form of prose. In some ways, it bears comparison with another long and hard-to-categorise work of Clive's, his eccentric 'verse commentary on Proust', *Gate of Lilacs* – half poem, half critical essay – which he published in 2016. *Gate of Lilacs* is presented as a fifty-page poem, written in blank verse. But it is seldom self-consciously poetic, and many of the most striking passages would pass for richly brilliant prose, if the lines had not been chopped up and laid out as verse. Proust's insight into youthful lust, for example, is summed up in a couple of neatly turned and conventionally grammatical sentences:

> The way he writes about desire reminds us
> Of what it was when we were still too young
> To know about its power, but everywhere
> We felt it, and in everything. The world
> Was soaked in it.

Poetry or prose, the distinction hardly seems to matter, though it clearly does to Clive. In the obituary for Diana, there are whole passages that could equally be laid out as poetry, and the richness and density of ideas is just as striking.

> She wasn't just beautiful. She was like
> The sun coming up: coming up giggling

When Charles and Diana were engaged in a PR war ('Diana's people were busy calling Charles a stuffed shirt, and Charles's people were just as busy calling Diana a dingbat'), Clive had to make it clear that he couldn't say a word against the prince, in public or in private.

> I told her that if we were caught talking high treason she would be
> given the privilege of dying by the sword, whereas I, a commoner and
> a colonial, would be lucky if they even bothered to sharpen the axe.

The joke is founded on historical fact, with its reference to Anne Boleyn, who, because of her royal status, was spared the axe and beheaded with a single stroke by an expert swordsman brought in from France for the purpose. But you don't need to know about Henry VIII's second wife to enjoy the wit and energy of the writing.

Throughout Clive's tribute to Diana, he declares his love for her (though he confesses it was 'too much love for so tenuous a liaison, and one of the reasons I never spoke of it in public was a cheaper fear – the simple, adolescent fear of appearing ridiculous'). But he offsets this with realism ('on a hair-trigger, she was unstable at best') and a full awareness of how he, like so many others, allowed himself to be influenced as she tried to recruit the sympathies of various prominent media figures. 'It was manipulation,' he wrote. 'But what else does a marionette dream of except pulling strings?' When it came to talking about Andrew Morton's 1992 biography, *Diana: Her True Story*, which was based on a series of taped interviews and revealed her bulimia and self-harming, her five suicide attempts and Charles's adultery, she looked him straight in the eye and lied in her teeth. 'I really had nothing to do with that Andrew Morton book,' she said.

Considering when it was written, in the swirling emotional aftermath of Diana's passing, Clive's lament presents a remarkably balanced assessment of her strengths and failings. Feelings were running high, and troubled speculation about the manner of her death coloured people's view of her life and character. During those first days and weeks, everyone was confused and suspicious about how the crash had happened and who was to blame for killing the princess. Had the paparazzi who chased the car on their motorbikes caused the tragedy? Was the driver, Henri Paul, drunk, or had he been poisoned? What had happened to the mysterious white Fiat

Uno that may, or may not, have collided with the black Mercedes as it entered the Alma tunnel – and that then seemed to vanish off the face of the earth? Had MI6 or the CIA or Mossad or the French security services been involved? Why was it an hour and twenty minutes before the ambulance set off for the Pitié-Salpêtrière Hospital – and why did the 3.8 mile journey take 25 minutes?

Conspiracy theories were rife. Maybe the princess had been murdered because she was about to marry Dodi or because she was pregnant with his child. Maybe she had been assassinated because of her high-profile campaigning against the use of landmines. For the next ten years, Dodi's father, Mohamed Al Fayed, claimed, loudly and insistently, that Dodi and Diana had been killed by MI6, on the orders of the Duke of Edinburgh. Her death seemed so cruel, sudden and arbitrary that people couldn't bring themselves to believe it was a straightforward traffic accident.

But that is what it was. There was no conspiracy. The final inquest into the deaths of Diana and Dodi was not completed until April 2008, more than ten years later, but it was scrupulously thorough. The Operation Paget Report, prepared for the inquest by Lord Stevens, a former Metropolitan Police commissioner, presented 832 pages of evidence and interviewed 330 witnesses, including two new eye-witnesses. The inquest itself lasted 94 days and heard from 278 witnesses. The jury's verdict was that the victims had been unlawfully killed, that the crash was caused or contributed to by the grossly negligent driving and alcohol-impaired judgement of Henri Paul, by the speed and bad driving of the following vehicles and by the fact that the three people who died were not wearing seatbelts.

As the evidence emerged, it had become clear that it would have been quite impossible for any conspirators to have arranged to set a trap and ambush the car, as the vehicle, the driver, the route and the point of departure (from the back of the Ritz Hotel, rather than the front) had all been changed in the last hour or so before the crash.

After writing his original requiem for Diana, Clive followed it up a couple of years later with an equally thoughtful and substantial postscript, which was published in his essay collection, *Even As We Speak*. Since then, he has stopped writing about her and even tended to avoid talking about their friendship in interviews. But he has returned to the subject recently, in two short poems that appear together in his 2017 collection, *Injury Time*.

'*Sunt lacrimae rerum*' makes the emotional link between a dead girl's plastic duck seen sitting incongruously amid the filth and squalor of a disease-ridden Brazilian slum and Diana's 'lost earring found inside the crumpled dashboard of a crushed Mercedes'. The two objects, each surviving in an unexpected setting after the death of its owner, remind him of the immortal Latin phrase, first used by Virgil in the *Aeneid*. Aeneas weeps as he stares at a mural depicting the battles of the Trojan War and the deaths of many of his dearest friends. 'Sunt lacrimae rerum et mentem mortalia tangunt,' he says. Interpretations of this line vary wildly, but the standard version would be something like, 'There are tears in [*or* of] things, and mortal things touch the mind.' Seamus Heaney, a Virgil scholar as well as a poet, translated 'Sunt lacrimae rerum' as 'There are tears at the heart of things.' In Ian McEwan's *Machines Like Me*, the fictionalised Alan Turing glosses it as 'There are tears in the nature of things.'

This simple, sad, uncomplicated little poem, a mere eight lines of unrhymed blank verse, consists of just three sentences, two of them (translating the famous speech from Virgil) making up the first line. The connection that links the two images – the plastic duck and the princess's earring – is entirely personal to Clive, as no-one else would have made the association between them. The duck comes from his own direct experience, while the jewellery, a gold, bean-shaped earring, dented by the impact and missing its clasp, was found by the French forensic team several weeks after the crash and first reported by Reuters in late October 1997. In his note on the poem in *Injury Time*, Clive tells the story of filming in the *favela* in Rio and the savage fate of his team's local fixer, who splashed out a chunk of his fee on a pair of flashy white shoes and was duly murdered for them. 'The extreme tonal range of that city has haunted me ever since,' he writes, and that haunting memory may have triggered a connection with Paris, La Ville-Lumière, City of Light, city of lovers and, here, city of random and capricious tragedy. For me, the one word that stands out as especially powerful occurs in the sixth line, where Clive says 'the image makes me blink'. 'Blink' is not what we would expect. We might have been waiting for 'weep' or 'grieve', but 'blink', with its implications of numbness and the struggle to hold down a sudden pang of sorrow, is elegantly apt and understated.

The other poem about Princess Di, 'Choral Service from Westminster Abbey', is more conventional. It was published by *Prospect* magazine in 2015 and it recalls the funeral service, a huge public event, watched by thirty-two million television viewers in Britain and hundreds of millions around the world, in intimate, personal, impressionistic terms. For Clive, writing nearly two decades later, the ceremony remains an achingly raw emotional experience, though his memory has played tricks on him when it comes to the details of what actually happened. He is convinced he remembers the choir singing 'I Know Not the Hour', but that was not among the hymns sung at the abbey. He remembers six soldiers shouldering the coffin, but it was actually carried by eight young Welsh Guardsmen, who visibly struggled with the weight of the quarter-tonne lead-lined casket.

When it comes to describing the atmosphere of the occasion, though, Clive's gift for precise and evocative detail comes to the fore, with an unexpected focus on the sounds. As the choir sings 'May flights of angels sing thee to thy rest', the slow march of the coffin-bearers begins and the 'spit-shine parade boots' crunch on the flagstoned floor, then boom, whisper and eventually fade to silence as Diana makes her last exit, leaving the mourners to their thoughts and memories. This is clever. The gradual shift from the close-up immediacy of that word 'crunched' to the way the abbey's acoustics make the footsteps boom first, then whisper and die away creates a real sense of space, sidestepping the need for a more conventional visual description of the scene.

The unanswered question about Diana is still the same as it ever was. How much was hype, dazzle and projection and how much was real? In the last stanza, Clive tackles it head on: 'Her fantasy, or ours? I couldn't say.' The manipulation was real enough ('She pulled the names, she got them on her team'). There were political games going on, and she was consciously trying to build her personal brand. The phrase 'the People's Princess' was not her creation (it was coined by an Australian magazine in 1983, but later hijacked by Prime Minister Tony Blair, who used it when responding to the news of her death), while her own phrase 'I'd like to be a queen of people's hearts' was a deliberate bit of sloganeering that she first trotted out in her BBC TV interview with Martin Bashir in 1995. But these manoeuvres were just the froth. What mattered, Clive believes, were her actions: 'Think, though, of some crippled kid / She talked to a long time, and later on / Wrote letters to, and never said she did'.

Like most people who came into contact with Princess Di, he saw what she wanted him to see – and that probably included her weaknesses and foibles, as well as her charm and enthusiasm. His vanity was flattered by her confidences and indiscretions. She ran rings round him, when it suited her, and he was happy to be at the centre of those intimate, shared circles. For all her faults, he adored her. The sense of loss, encapsulated in the original lament and in the later poems, is almost tangible. Clive saw something unique in Diana, and he knew, when she died, that her memory would never leave him.

By the time of the crash, she had distanced herself from him and dropped him ('quietly and nicely') from her social list. He no longer fitted into the life she wanted to shape for herself, and he 'understood completely', knowing that there would be no more lunches, no more repeats of their one-crème-brûlée-and-two-spoons routine. For Clive, it was already all over. His *New Yorker* requiem, the week after her death, was published under the headline 'I wish I'd never met her'. But did he mean it? Did he really regret ever having known this

extraordinary, complicated, naive and ultimately doomed woman?
No. A thousand times, no.

Choral Service from Westminster Abbey

The Abbey choir sings 'I Know Not the Hour'
And once again we all sit silent where
She, only, was not sighing for the waste
Of youth, health, beauty and the *savoir faire*
That might have served us all well later on
Had there not been the panic-stricken haste,
The concrete tunnel and the car's crushed power,
Almost as if she wanted to be gone,

Even without the chance to say goodbye.
From my seat on the transept's left-hand aisle
I saw the ceremony end. Six men
Shouldered the coffin and I could have sworn
That they brought her to me. You well might smile,
But *she* could smile as if she were the dawn
All set for a night out. That she would die
So soon, and never race your heart again,

Seemed not in nature. Then the guards wheeled right
A yard in front of me, and their slow march –
Spit-shine parade boots on a flagstone floor –
Down the side corridor beyond the arch

Crunched, boomed and whispered and went silent. So
She started her flight home. It felt like theft.
Until she vanished few of us could know –
And now all knew, and nothing was more sure –

A light could die just from the way it shone.
Her fantasy, or ours? I couldn't say.
She pulled the names, she got them on her team:
No question. Think, though, of some crippled kid
She talked to a long time, and later on
Wrote letters to, and never said she did.
Tell yourself then that she was just a dream,
Gone when the soldiers carried her away.

Sunt lacrimae rerum

There are tears in things. Things mortal touch the heart.
On the *favela*, sitting in the paste
Of clay and urine, in the fever season
At the festering tip of a high-level Hades,
Is the plastic duck of a little girl who died
Of typhus, and the image makes me blink,
Recalling the lost earring found inside
The crumpled dashboard of a crushed Mercedes.

17

Under Fire

Clive's recent books of short verses, *Sentenced to Life* and *Injury Time*, and the massive *Collected Poems* (2016) have sold in huge numbers and generated enthusiastic reviews in Britain, the US and Australia. But there are some who just won't have it.

'The man's a brilliant highbrow parodist, a capable light verse writer, but he has never been and never will be a poet of interest,' wrote the splenetic critic of *Crikey*, a well-established Australian political website, in a 2009 article headed 'On the Awfulness of Clive James'. This apoplectic rant, sparked by the publication of one of Clive's poems in the *Australian Literary Review*, began by merely dubbing the poem 'self-parodic' and 'depressingly bad' but soon got into its stride.

Warming to its task, it accused Clive of 'great bad poetry' comparable with that of Alfred Austin, the late-Victorian Poet Laureate, known to his critics as 'the Banjo Byron', whose monument is his infamous couplet about the illness of King Edward VII: 'Across the wires, the electric message came: / He is no better, he is much the same.' *Crikey*'s assault was slightly weakened by a trivial factual inaccuracy (the monarch involved was Edward, and not, as stated,

George V), but the whole 650-word tirade managed to sustain an impressively shrill vitriolic pitch. To be fair, the same writer, returning in 2012 for a vicious *ad hominem* attack on Clive's morals, judgement and conduct, did reluctantly admit that his illness had 'produced a handful of good poems from him, spare and direct lyrics focused through the prism of imminent death'. No matter that prisms don't focus; at least he'd noticed that Clive had written some worthwhile poems.

Yet of all the insults hurled at his poetic output, by far the most acute is a line taken from a 1987 novel, *The Remake*, written (you may already have guessed this) by Clive himself. In the book, a minor character called 'Clive James' is introduced as a shambling, overweight jogger, a struggling freelance journalist and hand-to-mouth literary hack who 'writes poetry that sounds the way reproduction furniture looks'.

That, of course, is exactly the charge that would be levelled at Clive's poems by those who dislike them most, though few would have the wit to phrase it so neatly.

His harshest critics mock his fondness for traditional, old-fashioned rhymed verses and accuse him of using self-conscious literary allusions interspersed with arbitrary references to topical events and pop culture icons, larded with cheap sentimentality and ornamented with laboured punning and wordplay. They see these as a clutch of characteristics that mark him indelibly as a talented faker – a poetaster, rather than a real poet, an ingenious copyist whose output has all the hallmarks of poetry except the creativity.

If all this were true, there could hardly be a more precisely damning jibe than likening the poems to repro furniture. Indeed, it is a sign of Clive's self-knowledge and awareness that he came up with this disarmingly insulting label thirty years ago, and that it has never been bettered since. Having begun writing poems at university in Sydney in the late 1950s, he had already accumulated thirty years' experience by the time he wrote *The Remake*. In the decades that have passed since then, he has worked to refine his craft and develop subtleties of tone and emotional control that have raised his poems to new levels. But since his terminal illness began, he has also been brought face to face with experiences and ideas that have given him new perspectives and a new sense of urgency.

'I've always written poetry, and I like to think that I fluked the occasional good one,' he told the *Financial Times* in 2015. 'But nowadays, in this situation, I've got a lot to write about and I'm less likely to fool myself into thinking that a bad poem is a good one.'

As an astute literary critic, as well as a practising poet, Clive knows his own habits and vices well enough to keep them under control, though he can't always erase them completely. In his later poems, there is less evidence of the repro furniture tendency. But there are still elements that drive his detractors mad.

One especially hydrophobic critic, Justin Clemens, a lecturer at the University of Melbourne and a poet himself, finds two particular reasons to take issue with Clive. Despite sharing his family name with Mark Twain, he showed little mercy or finesse when he reviewed *Sentenced to Life* alongside Les Murray's 2015 collection, *Waiting for the Past*, in *The Monthly*, a respected Australian magazine that has published many of Clive's poems and reviews over the years. Starting off with a ridiculous attack on older men for being old (art, he explains, dismissively, is 'not an old man's game'), Clemens, fifty, soon drops some initial hints about his attitude to Clive and his work, accusing him of sinking into 'an often-bathetic sincerity', charging him with 'sentimentality and self-pity' and mentioning that he 'seems incapable of writing a line without trying to purple it up'.

But this is generalised knockabout stuff, compared with the major objections Clemens reveals. One of these is that what Clive writes isn't poetry for today.

'James doesn't seem to have taken in any new technique or idea since 1950,' he spits. 'It's just not contemporary poetry... Nor do you have to like contemporary poetry to be a part of it. But you do have to keep attending to that which you do not understand or favour. If not, you're lost.'

Leaving aside the weakness of the thesis that poetry is a progressively developing technology, inching forward, like computing, towards ever-better standards of performance, this is just silly. It is also more than a bit rich, coming from a writer whose best-known poem is *The Mundiad*, an interminable mock-heroic opus in Augustan rhyming couplets, full of clumsy scansion, forced rhymes and gratuitous pop culture references ('Where black-eyed boxes catch each sparrow's fall, / And our bright globe becomes a disco ball / Whose beams illuminate the meanest *rue*, / So that the thought "Now's Night" is *never* true'). Clemens is not marooned in the eighteenth century, though, and he proves it with 'Blind Spot', an eight-line nonsense poem, presumably inspired by Lear or Lewis

Carroll (or maybe by insane twentieth-century writers like Ernest Vincent Wright and Georges Perec, who both wrote whole 50,000-word lipogrammatic novels without using the letter 'e'). In 'Blind Spot', he has the bright idea of restricting himself to using only the letters b, l, i, n, d, s, p, o, t – and u and e. This poetic curio – it begins 'Slip id to lop its / nob, lost din on lip's nil boil...' – does not prove its author's commitment to contemporary poetry, any more than his other wilfully eccentric poems with titles like 'We Begin Building That Which Cannot Collapse Because It Will Have to Have Been Built As If It Had Already Fallen' and 'Ten Thousand Fucking Monkeys Are Blowing Me Trumpet'.

What this kind of Poundland poetry shows is simply that Clemens wants to insist on being seen as a radical. He's a clever man, a decent critic on his day, and he should know better. Those of us who lived through the sixties and seventies have seen this stuff before – and it didn't work then, either.

Clive may choose to write much of his own poetry within the formal disciplines of rhyme and metre, but he adores the free verse of Walt Whitman, the man he calls 'everybody's big influence'. ('Makes no sense at all on the formal level. Didn't intend to. Didn't want to. But he's always worth going back to, I find, especially as I get older.') And he has demonstrably been 'attending' to contemporary poetry for a long time. His taste is catholic and unpredictable. Alongside the beloved triumvirate of Yeats, Auden and Larkin, he likes Eliot and Louis MacNeice, Cummings and Elizabeth Bishop, the early John Ashbery and the late Michael Donaghy. He has been an enthusiastic supporter of Australian poets from several different traditions and generations, from Peter Porter and Les Murray to Philip Hodgins, Peter Goldsworthy, Judith Beveridge and Stephen Edgar. (Edgar, coincidentally, like Clive, was born in Kogarah and studied at Sydney Technical High School, though he was still in short trousers when the older man set sail for England. In his *Poetry Notebook*, James says of Edgar: 'His poems are more sheerly beautiful from moment to moment than those of any other modern poet I can think of.')

Clive's interest is always the same. It lies in finding what's fresh and wonderful, wherever it comes from and whatever form it takes. If his delights and influences don't show through explicitly in his poems, it is precisely because he has no interest in the kind of pastiche that would make such connections obvious.

The other main criticism levelled at Clive by Clemens – and by other Australian poets and academics over the years – is the assertion that he somehow betrayed his homeland heritage by making his life and career in Britain. In his review in *The Monthly*, Clive's assailant discounts the positive reaction to *Sentenced to Life* as mere backscratching, within a literary clique that presumably extends from the UK to both America and Australia. 'If one scans the unending laudatory reviews of James's poetry, the cronyism is palpable,' he says, making it clear that he sees Clive as 'a colonial pander' and one who was 'desperate to nestle into the armpit of a decaying English literary hierarchy'. Clemens had already had a similar swipe at his target in an earlier article in *Overland*, another Melbourne-based magazine, referring to Clive's 'dotage' being spent under the spell of his 'toadying appreciation of received Oxbridge opinions about "great writers"'. This is arrant nonsense, an argument that can only be based on a refusal to read Clive's real opinions, but this kind of loathing does not rely on facts.

Back with *The Monthly*, Clemens cannot resist the opportunity to pour scorn on Clive's UK television career – fifteen years, a hundred poems and ten books after it came to an end – and link it, tenuously, with his alleged refusal to pay attention to poetry's march of progress.

'Once upon a time, James would happily lap at the weirdest secretions of popular culture with gusto, but something in him just said "no" to the real developments in poetry.'

The temptation to let biographical detail dictate one's view of a poet's work is often irresistible. In this case, the assumption is that Clive's years in the media spotlight somehow made it impossible for him to recognise and respond to the poetry that was being written in the last two or three decades of the twentieth century.

But there is, of course, no logical connection between the two halves of Clemens's proposition. The fact that Clive made popular television programmes that featured Japanese game shows and the grotesquely watchable Margarita Pracatan ('She never lets the words or melody get in her way. She is us, without the fear of failure,' he once said) had nothing whatever to do with his ability to spot poetry's 'real developments'. Indeed, throughout his career, he has always been quick off the mark when a new poet arrives with something special to say. He was an early fan of Seamus Heaney (a distant cousin of mine, incidentally, on my mother's side). In the 1960s, he wrote enthusiastically, perceptively and anonymously – the *Times Literary Supplement* didn't believe in bylines back then – about

Heaney's ability to 'make the gesture that enlivens life', about his 'hard-edged technique' and his 'virtuoso kinetic gift'. More recently, he has championed younger compatriots like Philip Hodgins and Stephen Edgar and the Americans Michael Donaghy and Christian Wiman with a certainty and conviction that brooked no argument. If his own poems show a concern with form the more prescriptive modernists find infuriating, his generosity in recognising and drawing attention to the essential qualities of a successful poem, whatever its shape and idiom, has been consistent and enlightening. He even has a degree of sympathy for his attackers' point of view.

'I suppose it's hard not to classify me as a formalist,' Clive told me. 'I write in formal measures and I don't hesitate to mention the odd obscure name. So my poetry's got some of the furniture of learning – and that's thought to be anti-democratic by many of the young and more radical Australian poets. Most of them *are* radical, and that's fair enough. It's a radical country.'

In fact, though, if you were the sort of dull and pedantic plodder who could be bothered to sit and count these things, you'd find that more than a quarter of Clive's poems in *Sentenced to Life* and *Injury Time* are unrhymed.

I know. I've just done it. They include some of the best, too – 'Asma Unpacks Her Pretty Clothes' and 'Change of Domicile' in the earlier volume, 'Elephant in the Room', 'Not Forgetting George Russell', 'Aldeburgh Dawn' and the shorter of the two poems about the death of Princess Diana, 'Sunt Lacrimae Rerum', in *Injury Time*. There is also one of Clive's best long poems, 'The Rest Is Silence', about his wife, Prue Shaw, and their shared love of Beethoven, which begins with a three-verse rhymed introduction and follows on with another six sections in unrhymed iambic pentameters.

'Elephant in the Room' is a particularly interesting poem, ostensibly about the final scene in the life of a dying African bush elephant. Clive claims to remember the striking, unforgettable image of the elephant kneeling down to die from a television documentary many years ago ('probably an Attenborough programme' he says). But my necessarily limited research has failed to track down any film or even mentions of such an event and I have come to suspect that it is a picturesque metaphor conjured up by his fertile brain.

The idea of this mighty beast, with its legendary intelligence and its proverbial memory, dying in a kneeling position and being quietly hollowed out by ants and termites until 'There is only skin, draped thickly on its cage / Of bones' is certainly full of poetic potential. But even the poem's title is surely a hint that it should not be taken at face value. There is no room. The scene is set on the banks of a dried-up riverbed, somewhere on the African plains. And, in its normal idiomatic context, the elephant in the room, of course, means something else – the big issue that no-one wants to talk about or spell out.

The fact is that this poem, like almost all Clive's recent poems, is about his own situation. He has come to a place in his life from which he will go no further. His house in Cambridge is his river bank. He's still standing, just as the elephant, as it dies and afterwards, remains 'precisely balanced on its bended knees', though it's a 'shadow of its former self'. Clive is frail and vulnerable, kept going by a combination of drugs, nursing and willpower, but well aware, as he has been for years now, that his ruined body is poised on the edge of the abyss – 'A breath of wind will knock it down, an hour / Of rain wash it away'. He is the hollow man, the empty elephant, but he is still there, and still, remarkably, recognisably himself.

'Elephant in the Room' does not use rhyme. Its five six-line stanzas are modelled on the traditional English iambic pentameter, liberally interpreted, with both longer and shorter lines when necessary. It doesn't bear the outward signs of traditional formalist verse, and yet it is undeniably shaped and disciplined by a strict sense of metre. You can tell it's poetry, because you can't read it as prose. The diction is rhythmic, the wording terse and distilled, and the poem forces its shape and fluid movement upon you as you read, in ways that utterly disprove the sniping of Clive's most zealous critics.

Whatever else this is, it is not old-fashioned poetry that sounds the way reproduction furniture looks. It's supple, flexible and emotionally powerful, and it demonstrates Clive's ability to use a wide range of forms and techniques to create the effects he has in mind. There is a discipline at work here, but it is not the kind that limits and distorts the poem.

'The common assumption among a lot of Australian poets and academics is that if you embrace discipline, you give up your freedom,' says Clive. 'They believe free verse is a requirement of liberty, and anything constructed to a pattern must be leaving something essential out. I don't buy that. But I do understand where it comes from. It's a very Australian feeling, and it comes from somewhere deep in our character. Freedom is a sensitive issue, still – and no-one wants to wear the broad arrow of the convict suit.'

Elephant in the Room

On slow last legs it comes to the right spot
Near the dried-up river bed where it may kneel
And die. The plain is open, with one clump of trees
Parched, bleached, more grey than green,
Much like the grass:
The perfect setting for what happens next.

What happens next is nothing. Still upright,
Precisely balanced on its bended knees,
The elephant decays. All by itself
It loses its last flesh with neither vultures
Nor hyenas to help with the unloading:
They seem to have been paid to stay away.

When all the meat is gone
There is only skin, draped thickly on its cage
Of bones. Perhaps the ants are in there
Like vagrants in the ruins of New York.
There might be termites cleaning out its tusks.
If so, it shows no signs of pain or anger.

Through hollow eyes it looks out of the screen
With what seems an inflexible resolve.
The shadow of its former self has timed
Its exit to sum up what it did best,

To bulk large as a thing of consequence
Even though emptied of its history.

A breath of wind will knock it down, an hour
Of rain wash it away, but until then,
Sustained by stillness, it is what it is:
A presence, a whole area in space
Transformed into a single living thing
That now, its time exhausted, lives no more.

18

The People's Poetry

A couple of years ago, author and illustrator Gary Dexter gave up his work for health reasons and took to the streets to try an unusual experiment. His plan was to earn his living as a poetry performer, buttonholing people in pubs, shopping centres, parks and motorway service stations, wherever he found them, and inviting them to name their favourite poems. He had memorised a wide range of popular verses and he would recite any of them, on request, before passing a hat round. For a year, Dexter spent his time ambushing family groups and pensioners, sentimental drunks and shy students, bemused tourists and raucous football fans, tired shoppers, loving couples and innocent passers-by, building up a unique picture of the place poetry holds in the lives of ordinary people.

Street poetry is not part of people's everyday lives and Dexter's hit rate was low. Only one encounter in ten yielded money or an interesting conversation. More typical responses were either politely dismissive or menacingly resentful, reeking of class warfare, sore memories of unhappy schooldays, sneering animosity towards beggars and buskers or blankly motiveless malignity. Many people turned away, saying, 'Sorry, I've only got cards.' Others reacted with confrontational energy: 'Do I look like I know anything about poetry?' 'Piss off. Get a job!' 'If *I* tell *you* a poem, will *you* pay *me*?' 'Spit some grime.' 'Roses are red, violets are blue, your poems are shit, and so are you.' 'Fuck off.' Dexter soon became skilled at defusing ominous situations and knowing when to beat a rapid retreat. But he emerged from his year in the front line in one piece and with some remarkable insights into the state of the nation in relation to its poetic heritage.

The results of his street-level survey were fascinating. The same poems were requested again and again. By the end of the year, he could identify a Top 30 that reflected the reality of the public's taste and ranged from Keats and TS Eliot to Spike Milligan. But the public's favourite poem, the Top of the Pops and Dexter's greatest earner, by a clear margin, was Rudyard Kipling's 'If –'.

One minute long when spoken out loud, rhythmic and rhymed, it is stuffed full of Victorian values and sterling advice (at least until you reread it and start to think about what it actually says). People, men and women, would smile or cry, hug the performer as if he were the poet himself or join in with the thunderous last line, 'You'll be a Man, my son! in a kind of spontaneous poetry karaoke.

Most people don't like poetry, Dexter discovered, over the course of his year-long experiment. But most of those who do seem to find something to love in 'If –'.

The silver medallist could not have been more different. Apart from anything else, Philip Larkin's 'This Be the Verse' ('They fuck you up, your mum and dad…') is not the kind of poem that was traditionally rammed down children's throats in schools. Right from the first line, it announces itself as something too strong and disruptive for young minds, which, of course, makes it immensely attractive to them. As Dexter observes drily, 'The term "parental advisory" might have been coined for it, since it's a warning about parents.'

After Kipling and Larkin, the rest of the Top Ten continues to jump around between ancient and modern. Wilfred Owen's 'Dulce et Decorum Est' is in third place, followed by Wordsworth's daffodils, Robert Frost's 'Stopping by Woods on a Snowy Evening', Dylan Thomas's 'Do Not Go Gentle into That Good Night', Poe's raven, Blake's tyger, Auden's 'Funeral Blues' (otherwise known, especially to filmgoers, as 'Stop All the Clocks') and finally Shakespeare's Sonnet 18 ('Shall I Compare Thee to a Summer's Day?').

Just over twenty years ago, a BBC Radio 4 survey put together a Top 30 for a book called *The Nation's Favourite Poems*, edited by Griff Rhys Jones. 'If –' was top of that poll, too, but many others featured in the BBC's list – poems like 'The Lady of Shalott', Gray's 'Elegy' and Matthew Arnold's 'Dover Beach' – have sunk without trace, at least as far as people on the streets are concerned.

Generations age and go. Syllabuses change. Fashions shift. But there is more to it than that. Sampling a cross-section of people on the street, rather than the self-selecting Radio 4 audience, Gary Dexter uncovered a widespread sense of resentment and distrust of the very idea of poetry.

Hundreds of people reacted to his performances with joy and wonder, hugs and tears. Thousands more sidestepped his approaches, cut him off abruptly or tried to pick a quarrel. People don't like being accosted, but that was only part of the story:

And then there was the sheer hatred of poetry itself. People (some people anyway) were violently allergic to it. They'd had bad experiences at school. They didn't understand it. It was pretentious bollocks. It was laughable, embarrassing bollocks. It had nothing to offer in a world in which real things happened, such as death and babies and shagging. Never mind that these things were what poetry was about; it was about them in a way that occluded them.

And, he might have added, in a way that somehow excluded a lot of sane, intelligent, curious people who might otherwise have found the same kind of pleasures in poetry that they enjoy in music, novels, films and even TV series.

For Clive James, poetry has to be able to break through these barriers if it is to be relevant in the twenty-first century. It must not be like opera, an intensely stylised re-enactment of an antique spectacle, accessible only to the initiates.

It can be demanding, impressionistic, allusive, but it must not be patronising. As he says in his *Poetry Notebook*, a poem must create special moments: 'It's the moment that gets you in.' And when he insists, later on, that 'A poet who can't make the language sing doesn't start', he's getting close to the one thing all the poems in Gary Dexter's Top 30 have in common.

The great standout phrases – Stevie Smith's 'Not waving but drowning', Shelley's 'Look on my works, ye mighty, and despair', WE Henley's 'I am the captain of my soul', WH Davies's 'What is this life if, full of care…?', 'They fuck you up', 'Stop all the clocks' and 'Do I dare to eat a peach?' – all have that grapnel quality, snagging a place in the memory from which they cannot be dislodged.

Poetry's not just about glittering phrases, of course. There's rhythm and rhyme (of all the people's favourites Dexter was asked for, Charles Bukowski's 'Bluebird' was the only example of free verse) and the mysterious forward thrust and momentum that makes a great poem sound not just right but inevitable. There are ideas, images and emotions, too, the formal content of a poem. Yet people seldom remember whole poems, unless they have been forced to learn them by heart at school. What they remember are the shining fragments – what Clive calls 'the moments'.

Throughout his career, as a writer, critic, poet, lyricist and TV performer, he has demonstrated an extraordinary capacity for creating memorable moments. This is not just a matter of verbal ingenuity, the apparently effortless ability to mint a fresh and luminous phrase. It's to do with spotting connections, parallels and contrasts, binding ideas and insights together in startling images that make them fused and inseparable. When he mentioned Arnold Schwarzenegger's physique as looking like 'a brown condom full of walnuts', forty years ago, he made it impossible to think of Arnie without this graphically comic association. But even Clive has never been sure how this durable epigram came to be born.

'The idea must have been a registration of his bulges and skin texture,' he wrote in *North Face of Soho*. 'But I still don't know how the visual perception translated itself into a verbal creation.'

The condom full of walnuts was Clive wearing his journalism hat. But the same ability to forge a connection and beat it into a shining phrase is evident in all his work. His grossly neglected career as a lyricist, writing some two hundred songs in a fifty-year collaboration with his musical partner, Pete Atkin, has thrown up dozens of similarly epic moments. In one song about the golden days of Hollywood, he unleashes a reference that unexpectedly yokes together two great movie themes: 'Atlantis down in bubbles, / And Atlanta up in flames'. In another, about Elvis in Las Vegas, the King is described as sparkling 'like the frosting on a drumkit'. In 'The Wall of Death', the stunt rider challenges the narrator to show him what he's got: 'Take off your face, we'd like to see the mask.'

In his poetry, Clive has generally chosen to keep this flamboyant energy under control. It's there, of course, in comic poems like 'The Book of My Enemy Has Been Remaindered' and the early mock-heroic epics like *Peregrine Prykke's Pilgrimage*. And it occasionally surfaces in the more serious poems, though there is always the danger that the incandescent moment will unbalance and overshadow the rest of the poem.

In 'What Happened to Auden', for example, a sad and solemn assessment of the great man's decline, Clive embodies the very point he's making about his flawed hero in the opening of his own poem. The beginning, 'His stunning first lines burst out of the page / Like a man thrown through a windscreen', is so powerful that the poem seems to rock and reel for several stanzas before it regains its poise and finds its voice.

By the time it builds up towards its last crescendo, Clive is on top form again:

A mortal fear of talking through his hat,
A moral mission to be understood

> Precisely, made him extirpate the thrill
> Which, being in his gift, was his to kill.

This is followed by a remarkable line – 'He wound up as a poor old fag at bay' – that may seem to carry an outdated whiff of homophobia but is unquestionably resonant, the rhyming fag/stag echo evoking a harried and threatened nobility that seems exactly right. As the poem reaches its end, it becomes clear that Clive's respect and admiration for Auden's contribution to the twentieth century is undiminished by the doubts and lapses of his later years:

> But deep down he had grown great, in a way
> Seen seldom in the history of his art –
> Whose earthly limits Auden helped define
> By realising he was not divine.

The question is, though, whether the poem manages to survive the explosive, distracting impact of the man-through-a-windscreen and fag-at-bay images. I think it does, but only just. Those are undoubtedly the fragments that would remain lurking in the mind of any deep-dyed Clive James fan who was prompted to ask Gary Dexter, the poetry busker, for an ad hoc recital.

Ian Hamilton, Clive's long-time friend, editor and critical mentor, once described John Betjeman as 'accessible and shrewd and funny', but also as 'trippingly theatrical' and marred by 'an ingrained showmanship, a look-at-me predictability'. At its worst, when he veers into the glib and flippant, Clive's poetry has the same engaging weaknesses, though his use of language could never be called predictable. But even Betjeman himself was not as conventional as his cartoon image. His provocative 'Slough', written just three years before the first bomb fell on the town, revealed an unexpectedly bruising passion and social awareness, and there was more depth to him than he would ever let on. (He was even taught, at junior school in Highgate, by a young American teacher called TS Eliot, though the influence doesn't necessarily show through.)

Betjeman became too well known for his own good in the sixties and seventies, just as Clive did in the eighties and nineties, because of the double-edged blessing of television exposure. TV is not good for a poet's reputation. Once the face and voice become too familiar, the poetry is seldom given the benefit of the doubt. Anything remotely complicated or obscure is seen as trying too hard. Anything that seems too easy is quickly dismissed as doggerel or tagged with the damning label of 'light verse'.

In Clive's case, though, the habitual lightness of touch often hides a concern with major themes. One of the finest poems in *Injury Time* is 'Use of Space', which starts off talking about the results his granddaughter, Maia, has achieved in her junior dance examination and gradually develops into a gentle meditation on death and the way the baton is passed on to future generations.

The youngster's exam is judged section by section and she scores an impressive nine marks for Use of Space, prompting Clive to remember the carefree youth in which he, too, could imagine himself developing into a talented dancer. 'I thought of Dance as something I could do' he says. 'I never could, of course. I merely flung / Myself about with untrained feet and hair.' Maia has a talent her adoring grandfather – she calls him 'Gruncle' – could never aspire to. Though he has described her elsewhere as a girl who 'jumps everywhere like an ecstatic wallaby', she has the real dancer's ability, even at the age of nine, to rise above a stylised pattern of movements and attain a certain level of transcendence: 'I've seen / Her switch to different corners of the room / Without, it seems, crossing the space between'.

Clive's own Use of Space score has now fallen to zero. He hobbles painfully from desk to stairs and any travelling he does these days is by ambulance or wheelchair. The geography of his life, even within the little house in Cambridge, has already shrunk to almost nothing and it will come to an end, soon, with a 'collapse into a spill of dust'. But this conclusion, which could have been seen as anything but a happy ending, is not just inevitable ('timely, true and just'), but positive. It is part of the essential pattern and dance of life. For Maia and the members of her generation to live their lives and fulfil their potential, it is necessary for the old to let go. They must quit, when the time is right, vacating the space they occupy, releasing the resources they have amassed and opening up the world and its opportunities for those who are to follow. 'The old ones disappear, the young dance on,' the poem says. 'They use the space we make by being gone.'

'Use of Space' was largely overlooked by the reviewers when *Injury Time* came out in 2017. It had originally been published a year or so earlier in the *Literary Review*, under the glumly pedestrian title 'Modern Dance Certificate'. The text was identical, but for the ending. This was originally 'Using the space we make by being gone', a slightly anti-climactic line that became far more sonorous, satisfying and metrically pleasing when reshaped to complete a powerful closing couplet: 'The old ones disappear, the young dance on; / They use the space we make by being gone.' In its final form, this poem stands out as one of Clive's minor masterpieces, exactly the kind of short, plain-speaking lyric poem that could emerge as a popular favourite in times to come. For that to happen, though, it would have to be recognised and picked up by the anthologists and the other, less obvious, arbiters of the public's poetic taste.

There is really no mystery about how the people's favourite poems come to be so well known. They have to have something remarkable, some ringing, unique quality of form or content that stirs the apathetic and the poetry-haters and makes them prick up their ears. But they also have to be seen and heard, if they are to break out of the literary ghetto. They need to be printed and broadcast, anthologised and curriculated, quoted and misquoted, made visible in the day-to-day mainstream and, ideally, picked up and injected into the movies, stories and songs of popular culture.

Three of the poems in poetry busker Gary Dexter's Top 30 owe a large slice of their popularity to the fact that they were featured in much-loved films – Auden's 'Stop All the Clocks' in *Four Weddings and a Funeral*, Keats's 'Bright Star' in the film of the same name and 'The Life that I Have', by Leo Marks, in the 1950s WWII spy classic *Carve Her Name with Pride*. One of the two TS Eliot poems in the Top 30 is 'Macavity the Mystery Cat', which has had its immortality repeatedly renewed by the Andrew Lloyd Webber musical, *Cats*. (Eliot is the only poet with two works in the Top 30 list, though his other contribution, 'The Love Song of J Alfred Prufrock', presumably got there via a more conventional route.)

Charles Bukowski's 'Bluebird', written in 1992 and unknown to older generations but very popular with the young, has not had this kind of exposure. But Bukowski or his poem have been referred to in several songs by the Red Hot Chili Peppers, by the Arctic Monkeys ('She Looks Like Fun'), by U2 ('Dirty Day', on the *Zooropa* album, adapts a Bukowski line about the days running away like wild horses over the hills) and by Kasabian and The Boo Radleys.

Some of Clive's earlier poems have already been nudged into the limelight in ways that couldn't have been imagined in pre-internet times. 'Windows Is Shutting Down' ('and grammar are on their last leg') and the classic 'The Book of My Enemy Has Been Remaindered' often pop up in various social media channels, shared and enjoyed by a new generation of readers. 'Japanese Maple' became an online sensation in 2014 and has already caught the eye of the anthologists. But there are many more – including 'Manly Ferry', 'Early to Bed', 'Managing Anger' and 'Star System' from *Sentenced to Life* and *Injury Time*'s 'Anchorage International', 'Not Forgetting George Russell', 'Tactics of the Air Battle', 'Apotheosis at the Signing Table' and 'In Your Own Time'– that fully deserve to reach a wider audience.

Clive's naked ambition as a poet is a matter of public record. He wants to be taken seriously, though high seriousness in his work is often deflated by his fondness for a punning joke or a startlingly colloquial turn of phrase. He once accused Ezra Pound of being 'deaf to his own bum notes', but that's the sort of thrust that can all too easily be turned back on its author. Clive is arguably better as a critic than a poet. In his case, though, that's not too limiting, as he is quite extraordinarily talented in that department. And his critical acumen gives him a keen awareness of his rightful place in the pecking order.

'My ambition has always been to write a few really good, memorable poems,' he says. 'I would love to be known, after my death, as a fairly major minor poet.'

One obvious conclusion from the poetry busker's year reciting people's chosen poems on the street is that there is plenty of room in the public's affections for good poems by minor poets. The widespread antipathy towards poetry in general still leaves room for individual poems to make their mark – and nearly half of the popular favourites in Gary Dexter's Top 30 could be seen as proving the point that much-loved poems don't always come from the greatest poets. Given enough exposure in the media, the schoolroom and the anthologies, there are several Clive James poems that could potentially earn him the immortality he craves. Over time, 'Use of Space' may turn out to be one of them.

Use of Space

> My granddaughter has scored, for Modern Dance,
> Good marks in all departments, with a nine
> For 'Use of Space'. Give me another chance
> And her certificate might well be mine.
> I moved well at her age, and when I grew
> I thought of Dance as something I could do.
>
> I never could, of course. I merely flung

Myself about with untrained feet and hair.
No gift at all, except for being young,
And gradually that faded on the air
As I became another crumbling face
Scoring a pittance for his Use of Space.

Now I score zero. But because I've seen
Her switch to different corners of the room
Without, it seems, crossing the space between,
Delight reminds me time is a new broom:
It clears the floor our youngsters use to get
The compartmentalised certificate

That we'd have liked to have, but didn't put
The work into, and so did not deserve –
Although we might have been quite fleet of foot
And God knows that we would have had the nerve –
But we had other things to do and know.
Let her do this. Be glad, and let it go:

For you, the Use of Space comes to an end
With your collapse into a spill of dust,
And you are for the wind and waves, my friend,
And all of this is timely, true and just.
The old ones disappear, the young dance on;
They use the space we make by being gone.

19

The River in the Sky

In 2006, Clive James was interviewed for the *Sunday Times* by Bryan Appleyard. Clive had just brought out the fourth volume of his *Unreliable Memoirs* series, *North Face of Soho*, and was building up to the publication of *Cultural Amnesia*, his huge book about the vital and ambiguous connections between culture, politics and history. But in the course of their chat Clive mentioned several other projects he was lining up, including 'a multi-volume novel about the Pacific War, called *The River in the Sky*'.

'Beautiful phrase, that,' he told Appleyard. 'It's what the Japanese call the Milky Way. It's a great story. Australia and Japan were the two countries that knew least about each other in the world. That war consumed my father... and my mother.'

It was twelve years later that *The River in the Sky* finally arrived, in a much-changed form. It had metamorphosed from a three-decker novel into a vast, billowing 21 000-word poem and the focus had widened. It was no longer just about the war in the Pacific, though the shattering impact of his father's death in a plane crash on the way home from years spent in Japanese prisoner of war camps was still a major theme. It had become a verse autobiography of epic proportions and vaulting ambition, a revealing self-portrait, written by a dying man with an insatiable, undying urge to tell everything, make sense of everything and map the connections between the pinpoints of light that have illuminated his life.

Like all Clive's best writing, it is provocative, intelligent, curious, sometimes showy, often moving. It bubbles with enthusiasm for all those passions that have meant so much to him – love, beauty, music, family, travel, humour, literature, tango dancing, conversation, philosophy, military history and funfairs. It surges one way and another, sucking in experience, seeking patterns and paradoxes, trying to reconcile opposites and throwing off sparks like a knife-grinder's wheel.

His range of allusions is preposterous. You'd need to be a Jonathan Miller or a Daniel Kahneman, a Stephen Fry or a latter-day Leonardo, just to keep up with all the people and that places go flitting by, as the stream of references to classical myths, historical figures, authors, poets, cricketers, architects, scientists and Olympic diving medallists broadens out to include scenes from wildlife documentaries and YouTube videos of jazz and opera. In fact, of course, no-one but Clive can truly hope to follow every train of thought that snakes across his field of vision.

If you don't have memories of looking across Sydney Harbour at the faded remains of the Luna Park fairground, the bizarre grin of an enormous, gaudily painted plaster clown with entrance turnstiles studding his mouth will not mean much. But to Clive, sitting and writing at a table outside Rossini's café on Circular Quay ('only a month before my health broke down') and recalling the yearly visits that formed a highlight of his wartime childhood, Luna Park is a potent symbol of a lost world. He remembers the raw young servicemen he used to see there, enjoying their leave before heading off to the savagery of the Pacific battles. Their innocence, and his, are captured in a passage so vivid you can almost smell the adrenaline.

> …My mother took me there
> When the war was not yet over, and I saw
> Soldiers dive down the hill-high slippery dips
> In the hall called Coney Island – no-one knew
> The name was a cheap import – heavy-booted
> Surfers in uniform on wooden combers
> In flight above the bumps, gripping their thin
> Slick mats, harbingers of the boogie-board.
> Young couples, queuing for the River Caves,
> Nuzzled each other's faces. Why was that?
> Vaguely I guessed that the whole adult world
> Must feel far different to the people in it,
> Even in here, where they behaved like children.

The references come at you from all directions. If you don't know Netrebko and Garanca's 'Flower Duet' from *Lakmé* (otherwise known as the British Airways ad tune) or the grainy clip of Bill Evans playing 'Round Midnight' at his Stockholm concert in 1970, you can find them easily enough by plugging into what the poem calls 'YouTube's vast cosmopolis'.

If you are not familiar with the painters and the pictures Clive refers to, or the Egyptian gods and Hollywood screen goddesses he mentions ('Osiris… chic as Louise Brooks'), Google can help you out in a matter of seconds.

But *The River in the Sky* is not about flaunting an almost superhuman capacity for remembering and associating cultural reference points. Clive's much-loved contemporary, Les Murray, once summed up his friend's daunting omniscience and elephantine memory with the phrase 'Clive knows everything.' To which others, less kindly, might add, '…and he wants to make sure you know it'. That's not what this poem is doing, though. It is a genuine autobiography, an attempt to make sense of his life and times without the protective carapace of irony and humour that shields his privacy and guards his insecurities throughout the jaunty bestselling volumes of his *Unreliable Memoirs*. It's the same life, and he tells the same story. But this is a reckoning, rather than a review of past follies.

Don Paterson, Clive's editor at Picador, worked with him for more than two years to bring *The River in the Sky* to fruition. He calls it 'his grave-goods poem', the literary equivalent of the strange assortments of jewellery, tools, weapons, tokens and even much-loved pets that were customarily buried alongside dead heroes from prehistoric times to the late mediaeval period. In many cultures, this was to do with preparing for the journey to the afterlife. But Clive, faced with the last great temptation, holds steadfastly to his belief that there is no journey and no afterlife.

'No, of course there's no beyond. This is beyond. We're already there,' he told a startled interviewer from his least-favourite newspaper, the *Daily Mail*, a couple of years ago. Clive is the man, after all, who famously described religion as 'an advertising campaign for a product that doesn't exist'. Even at death's door, he has the courage of his lack of convictions.

And maybe this is custom too, when I
Give credit to my gathered images
As if they might come with me,
And you, too, come with me
Just as if the afterlife
Were life itself.

But no, there is no journey,
There never was a journey

The 'you', here and throughout the poem, is Prue, his wife. *The River in the Sky* is dedicated to her and she is one of the two dominant figures in this long narrative, a constant presence and an unfailing source of love and inspiration from Clive's early days as a student to these last long years of his physical decline.

We see Prue, 'a very fine example of a young Australian woman', before they were married, taking Clive into the privileged inner sanctum of a tower in Venice to savour page after page of wondrous illustrations in the sixteenth-century *Breviaro Grimani*. We see them together, enjoying the music they've shared over the decades – from The Supremes and Thelonious Monk to Beethoven sonatas and Puccini's *Manon Lescaut*, as performed by Placido Domingo and Mirella Freni. And here is Prue again, showing the side of her that Clive loves best, projecting her own fierce integrity onto the world around her: 'Honest, she thinks the world is honest too.' It's a mosaic, made up of tiny glimpses and Impressionistic dabs of colour, but the portrait is subtle, intimate and heartfelt.

The other key figure, though, is the father Clive never knew. Sergeant Albert Arthur James was held captive, enslaved and beaten in a Japanese POW camp throughout the early years of Clive's childhood and killed by a brutally ironic twist of fate when the American plane giving him a lift home a week after the end of the war crashed in a typhoon in Manila Bay.

Unlike the *Unreliable Memoirs* books, *The River in the Sky* is a highly personal autobiography, rather than a public one. Clive has lived his working life among the good, the great and the guilty, but the cast list for this long poem is almost devoid of borrowed lustre. There are no mentions of Katharine Hepburn or Princess Diana, Peter Porter or Germaine Greer, Johnny Rotten, Hugh Hefner or Roman Polanski, or the hundreds of other media celebrities, literary figures and academics he has known, interviewed or had public spats with over the years. There are short scenes involving the conductor Georg Solti and the choreographer Kenneth MacMillan, and Elle Macpherson makes a brief cameo appearance, when Clive finds himself sitting next to her on a flight from Singapore to Perth ('Fame has its privileges / And most of those are drawbacks / But now and then you get to breathe / The aura of the angel'). Apart from these three, and his friend, the influential theatre critic Kenneth Tynan (immortalised as the first man to say 'fuck' on BBC television), no star names are dropped.

Most of the characters are ordinary people, ranging from teachers and shopkeepers remembered from his remote childhood to his friend Shaista Tayabali, a young Indian-born blogger, poet and lupus sufferer he has got to know over the years of desperate and uncomfortable treatment they have both endured in the infusion clinic at Cambridge's Addenbrooke's Hospital.

Shaista is in her early thirties, but she has already been close to death several times. She has nearly lost her sight and she's been through a twenty-year odyssey of pain and disability that has helped Clive gain new perspectives on the nature of suffering.

> One day, to disabuse me
> Of my sentimental faith
> That all would be well for her
> – She being beautiful, I thought
> Damage would be undone
> By one of those divine rules
> That I know do not exist –
> She held back an eyelid so that I could see
> The bleb that held one of her eyes in place

The shining metal bleb, inserted by surgeons in an effort to ward off glaucoma and blindness, is a stark reminder that Shaista's lupus (an aggressive, unpredictable auto-immune disease, 'the wolf that runs at random') is an ever-present shadow, a constant, hydra-headed threat.

But it is in the flashbacks to his own early years that we see glimpses of the forces that shaped Clive's destiny. In one fantasy sequence, set in the old funfair at Luna Park, he meets his infant school teacher, Miss Coleman, who was quick to spot the timid child's talent and rewarded him for his efforts with privileged access to the one-roomed weatherboard school's coveted building bricks. 'Your quickness with / The words left me with no alternative / But to confer on you First Choice of Blocks' she says.

Another teacher, Old Mr Slavin (pronounced 'Slave-in', he recalls), is remembered as smiling 'even when he caned me' and lives on in Clive's memory as the first man he ever met who 'could put his words together, when he spoke, as if they had been written'.

His most influential teacher, though, was another schoolmaster, Mr Leonard, who inspired the kids with the neat athleticism of his back somersaults off the diving board. He was a war hero, too. He had been a navigator on the Lancaster bombers over Germany. But he, of course, had come back. 'A terrific teacher,' Clive says of him, 'so why, till now, have I always left him out, except for the occasional fleeting name-check?' It's almost too painful to put into words.

> The answer is too easy and still too daunting.
> The ideal father figure, he raised the question,
> Simply by being there, of what life would have been
> Like if my father had come home...
>
> The secret of the effort I have put
> Into forgetting him for these three quarters
> Of a century has to be he was so clearly
> The answer to my wish.

The young Vivian – his mother eventually allowed him to choose the name he wanted, after he got fed up with being stuck with a name that was usually used for girls – was there when the telegram arrived with the news of his father's death. It was a few weeks before his sixth birthday and he witnessed his stricken mother's anguish and desolation. From that point on, the rest of his childhood was played out against the background of her inconsolable grief and his own indelible feelings of guilt, as if he, at the age of five, had somehow been responsible for this arbitrary and inexplicable tragedy.

Graham Greene once said his aim, when writing about his youth, was to tell the story 'without irony or hindsight'. Clive's *Unreliable Memoirs* are awash with comic irony and knowing hindsight, but all that grandstanding is discarded here, in favour of a simple plotting of a post-war childhood in New South Wales. He swims, reads and has nosebleeds. When he feels 'the heat of a girl's palm', after the Church Fellowship social, it leads to his first tentative sexual experience. When Ashton's circus comes to town, he kisses the girl in the gold leotard, only to find, the next day, that the circus has moved on.

This is Australia, so sport plays its part, too. Clive feels his age when he recalls seeing legendary cricketing heroes: 'When I tell Australians now / That I saw Keith Miller play / They realise how old I am: / Like being there for Troy'. A few years later, a day spent watching the terrifying West Indian fast bowler Wes Hall at the Sydney Cricket Ground offers a potential lesson for a young poet.

At the SCG
Some genius timed his question
Exactly right as Hall

Strode back for his endless run:
'You going home, Wesley?'

I should have guessed right then
It's a sufficient destiny
To make the right remark
At exactly the right time:
A poem might be more than that
But it is never less.

Memories and images from the early days in Sydney become gateways to ideas that Clive will explore many years later. The old steamship that shuttled across the harbour between Circular Quay and Manly was a strange, push-me-pull-you creature, with bows at both ends so it could dock without turning. This 'double-ended ferry' is the perfect vessel for this voyage back into the past: 'The journey through the mirror / On the old *South Steyne* / To where I am now / In the valley of reflections / That fuse and then dissolve'.

The mirror and the reflections are key themes, as optical images occur throughout the poem. This is a life brought into close-up by a telescope, examined under the microscope, transmuted and thrown into unexpected patterns by kaleidoscopic doublings and visual echoes.

The central tragedy, the death of Clive's father on the flight back from his time as a prisoner of war in Japan, is associated with icons of circular motion. The image of 'The B24's propellers / Churning the sunlight on Okinawa / For the flight meant to bring / My father

222

home' finds parallels in the still-spinning wheel of the crashed car that launched Camus on his final journey into non-existentialism, in waterwheels, turnstiles and roulette wheels, and in the spiralling Andromeda Galaxy M31, 2.5 million light years distant and heading towards us at 68 miles per second, that is fated, eventually, to wipe out our own Milky Way.

Throughout *The River in the Sky*, stories and themes are nested, a story within a story, a theme within a theme within a theme. This is life as we actually recollect it, fragmentary, out of sequence, episodic, a story shaped by associations rather than chronology as Clive goes 'sailing on the stream of thought'. The tangled skein of personal memories is shot through with glimpses of insight into life's little mysteries, many of them to do with our relationship with the natural world. Why, for example, are we hard-wired to respond so positively to numerousness, the 'many-ness' of 'a zillion wildebeest' or 'a sea of kangaroos'?

> There must be somewhere in the mind
> A mechanism fine-tuned to remember
> Numerousness…
> Mass rallies of meerkats, torrents of field mice,
> Those penguins of the Antarctic islands
> That pour themselves into the booming ocean…

The pouring penguins, massed meerkats and flooding field mice are wonderfully evocative images, and there are many others that create an Attenborough-like aura of hushed wonder and unflagging curiosity.

223

The hermit crabs clamber their way up the housing ladder as they grow. The ostriches have the loping gait of long-distance runners. But why are the denizens of the ocean deeps always so nightmarishly ugly, when there is no light for them to see each other by?

A bag of warts kept open by long teeth,
Some star turn in the benthic horror show,
Hideous for no reason one can see
For they don't glimpse each other from the night
Of birth through all their stygian nights
Until they die.

People, places and ideas come at us from all directions, flickering across the screen of memory, jostling for attention. The Everly Brothers sing 'the way two seagulls / Would sing if they could charm the waves'. Himalayan snow leopards 'dive to the next cliff face / Where the ibexes find footholds / The size of coins'. The carnival city of Rio de Janeiro burns in his mind, its inexpressible, untranslatable glory seared on his retina ('River of January / Your beauty still destroys me, Rio').

The individual moments and film-like sequences cascade through the poem. Clive is moved by the sight of Hemingway's moccasins in his house in Cuba and by the vibrant blue that 'fills the flutes in the gold mask of Tutankhamun'. He is shaken by his own escape from a lunging crocodile and thrilled by Mark Knopfler's melodies on the early Dire Straits albums ('the guitar lick weary with its beauty'). He notes that nuclear blasts, filmed from above, look exactly like the jellyfish that pulsed in the water as his younger self waited to dive from the high board at the Sans Souci baths. He remembers being startled to learn that the Concorde airliner he was flying in grew 30cm longer as the friction heated it up in supersonic flight. It's an idea that has stuck with him: 'And now I find my life / Is like that, taking far more space / As it speeds towards the end'.

In the short lyric poems of his last two collections, *Sentenced to Life* and *Injury Time*, Clive has largely steered clear of starburst phrases and showstopping images. His tone has generally become less extravagant, in keeping with his recurring themes of death, illness, family, regret and nostalgia, and his concern for the shape and impact of the poem as a whole. In this last long poem, however, he has taken his foot off the brake. No-one can possibly read or remember a 120-page epic as a single experience, and the rules are different.

The River in the Sky is huge: at just over 3900 lines, it is considerably longer than *Beowulf* or Tennyson's *Maud*, though, of course, a mere trifle compared with the 10000 lines of *Paradise Lost*. And if a poem that will take up a lot of the reader's time is going to succeed, it must create memorable moments. *Maud*, with its convoluted storyline and absence of bright and quotable lines, is both too melodramatic and too dull for today's audience. (Even at the time, in the 1850s, an unkind critic condemned it as having one vowel too many in the title, adding, somewhat cattily, that it didn't matter which of the vowels you chose to delete.) *Beowulf* is incomprehensible to most of us. But *Paradise Lost*, far too long and far too religious to chime with today's tastes, still throws up remarkable phrases and images that lodge in the brain. 'Better to reign in Hell than serve in Heaven' and 'Our reason is our law' have a pithy directness that sounds surprisingly modern, while psychology and religion come together in lines like 'The mind is its own place, and in itself / Can make a Heaven of Hell, a Hell of Heaven.'

The River in the Sky is not trying to be *Paradise Lost*. Clive has never believed it's his job to test the reader's patience, and he knows what Samuel Johnson said of Milton's masterpiece, that 'none ever wished it longer'. His own epic began to take shape when he realised that 'a sheaf of unfinished poems belonged together' and that this accumulation of handwritten notes was adding up to something that told a coherent story, 'the story of a mind heading into oblivion'. Within a loosely autobiographical free verse framework, there are anecdotes and reflections, memories and jokes, changes of form and pace – even, at one point, near the end, a brief and unexpected shift into formal rhyme.

The challenge, in *The River in the Sky*, is to keep people plugged in and interested, and the moments of brilliance come thick and fast, jumping out at you, vivid and unexpected. Olympic divers are like 'hydraulic drills' as they pierce the water. Geese 'put their flaps down and wobble down to land'. Vinyl records are back in fashion 'As if burning cakes of peat / Were once again the chic / Way of making fire.' The bird feeder in Clive's garden is full of meal worms 'who possibly made an error / By allowing that tag to be hung on them'.

A lot of the best bits are about music – from Bill Haley and the Beach Boys to Miles Davis and Charles Mingus. Richard Strauss advises young conductors 'never to look at the trombones' as it 'only encourages them'. Thelonious Monk's "Round Midnight' is his 'most elemental thing: / Most beautiful and most bewildering / Because it builds a framework out of freedom'. Clive comes back to the same topic later: 'Monk couldn't blur / The structure of a tune carved out of fog / Because it is a blur already, / Like a mist by Turner full of different / Thicknesses of rain.'

And so it goes on – a torrent of ideas, asides and insights, an intriguing scrapbook of images and afterthoughts from a man who is interested in everything and always eager to share his enthusiasms with anyone who will listen. This is Clive straddling two horses at once, as Poet and Entertainer. It's a hard act to pull off, but he's been doing it for a literary lifetime and half the fun lies in the tension – and occasional tumbles – as we watch the performance unfold.

The underlying structure that drives this epic review of a lifetime's thoughts and experiences is almost imperceptible at first reading. We just have to trust our guide and go with the flow. But gradually, on closer acquaintance, it starts to take shape and seem less randomly organised. Through all the excursions and diversions, it broadly follows the course of Clive's life, from his fatherless childhood in the outer suburbs south of Sydney to his final days in the little house in Cambridge. In between, we see him make his way via journalism and television to a jetsetting lifestyle that takes him to the four corners of the globe, before he steps off the treadmill, coming home to his family and his books. His way with words, that old ability to 'turn a phrase until it catches the light', has always been his trademark, and even now, stripped of his health and vitality, he finds, almost to his surprise, that he just can't stop writing.

Towards the end of *The River in the Sky* there's a remarkable three-stanza, thirty-line poem, an island of rhyme in an ocean of free verse. It begins with the wonderful, sonorous line 'This is my autumn's autumn', which stirs memories of John Donne's "Tis the

227

year's midnight, and it is the day's' from his 'Nocturnal Upon St. Lucy's Day'. This three-verse sequence had already been picked out and published in the *TLS* as a standalone poem, under the title 'Occupation Gone', before *The River in the Sky* was unleashed.

In the poem, Clive sees himself coming to the end of a long career of writing for print and remembers the way the printing union members in Fleet Street kept up the old tradition of 'tapping out' their retiring colleagues by drumming out a farewell tattoo as they walked away, for the last time, from the busy noise of the Linotype machines and the rumbling presses.

His output has shrunk, he says, as, 'drained of strength', he can only fill his notebook 'at the rate of forty lines a year'. This may be seen as a slight poetic exaggeration, as Clive has produced ten books since he fell ill in 2010, writing three volumes of poems since 2015 and showing a determination and stamina most of us can only envy. But even though he feels the end of his career approaching, he still hears, however faintly, 'the music of the syllables'.

Unlike Othello, whose occupation's gone the moment he believes Desdemona's betrayal makes it impossible for him ever again to lead an army, Clive's identity does not depend on reputation. As long as he can hear the music, he can still step out and dance. There'll be no more field trips to exotic destinations, no more supersonic flights or tango lessons in Buenos Aires or interviews with A-list celebrities. The research phase is over. But, as *The River in the Sky* demonstrates, there's still a world of experience to explore and connections to be made in the crowded nerves and synapses of that richly stocked and ever-curious brain.

Occupation Gone (from *The River in the Sky*)

This is my autumn's autumn. Claiming the use
Of so much splendour with my failing eyes
I take it as a sympathetic ruse
To glorify the path of one who dies
And see him out of the composing room,
The way the printers tapped out a farewell
For someone walking to a silent doom
After a life of noisy work done well
Among the old machines. So he moves on:
Othello, with his occupation gone.

He made that huge mistake about his wife
Because he listened to a chief of staff
Who saw no future in his master's life
That might include a decent battle. Laugh?
I tried to, as I left my main event,
Which was to write for print. Now, if I must,
Some bitching lyric about where time went
Is all I get done, a fate merely just
For someone drained of strength. This notebook here
Filled at the rate of forty lines a year.

But this much I can do. I can, with care,
Make every line count, and perhaps, some day,
Light on an argument that takes the air
As used to happen when I had my say

With ease. What once I could command at will,

The music of the syllables, has run

And hidden, but deep down I hear it still,

The same way I can see the autumn sun

Behind the screens of leaves, still shining through

As good as gold, as beautiful as you.

20

Signing Off

As physical disability has narrowed the boundaries of Clive's world, the man who used to spend half his time darting around the globe has been brought down to earth with a bump.

For thirty years, he was rarely at home. There was always a stage, a studio or an audience waiting to hear from him. 'I packed a hold-all and went anywhere / They asked me' he wrote in one of his recent poems, 'Landfall'. 'I would cross the world by air / And come down neatly in some crowded hall'. But this compulsive jet-setting was more than just a matter of earning a living. It was an endorsement of his identity, a confirmation of his international importance and desirability, a physical acting-out of his insatiable curiosity. As the poem makes clear, he loved both the adulation of his eager fans and the edge of surprise and uncertainty that went with the lifestyle.

> It might have been a kind of weightlessness,
> That footloose feeling always on the brink
> Of breakdown: the false freedom of excess.

The crash landing brought about by his illness brutally changed all that, and changed his perspective. What once looked like strength and energy and purposeful intensity was a mirage. What's left after the mirage has faded is a bleak realisation of his vulnerability and the sacrifices, not always his own, that were required to keep up the illusion. It's a harsh awakening, but he takes it on the chin with disarming humility. 'I was born weak and always have been weak' he says, in the last stanza of 'Landfall'. 'I am here now, who was hardly even there.'

He will never revisit Australia. He will probably never see London again. When his big volume of *Collected Poems* was published, in summer 2016, the launch event was held in Pembroke College, a few hundred yards from his Cambridge home. The journalists, along with the illustrious guests, the Marrs, Stoppards, Tomalins and Frayns, all had to be brought up from London by coach.

As things stand now, the geography of his remaining time has shrunk to a few square miles. There are trips to Addenbrooke's Hospital for check-ups, operations and routine treatments ('I go there every three weeks and they replace my immune system through a hole in my arm'). But, like anyone who has borne the discomforts and indignities of having bits of machinery 'the size of combine harvesters' inserted vertically into his body, he is probably entitled to believe there is little else that life can show him. Having heard 'the thrumming howl of approaching farm machinery' at such close (and hind) quarters and come out smiling, he takes what pleasures he can from the injury time he has been granted. On bad days, there is little to do but reading, writing and resting. On good days, there is the prospect of setting forth in his lightweight high-tech wheelchair and getting a brief glimpse of the river, the grass and the people. But the nonchalant dynamism of the world traveller is gone for ever.

When I visited Clive again in the run-up to Christmas 2017, not long after his encounter with the combine harvester, he was on good form. Pummelled, bruised and half deaf, he was still puckishly entertaining, though he had been hard at work on the sixth and last volume of his bestselling *Unreliable Memoirs*, urged on by both his wife and his publishers.

'Prue keeps telling me to get on with it,' he explained. 'She insists I've still got a lot to write about. And she's right, but they're all mental events now, rather than physical ones. I can't go anywhere.'

The publishers, he said, had been clever about it, putting him under contract to write the final volume. He couldn't die without fulfilling that commitment, and he was fantasising about the underhand methods they might employ to ensure the book was completed.

'I know what they're up to. I suspect them of sending their special agents to steal into my bedroom at night and shove a needle in my arm, using secret drugs to keep me alive and kicking, whether I like it or not. They won't let me go until I've delivered the manuscript.'

During the globetrotting years, Clive did much of his work from book-lined flats he owned in London, first in The Barbican and later by the Thames at Butler's Wharf. But the family home was always in Cambridge. One way and another, the city has been his base ever since he talked his way into the university in the mid-1960s. He studied everything except what he was meant to be reading, became deeply involved in the Cambridge Footlights, wrote for all the university magazines, achieved a somewhat disappointing

2:1, led the Pembroke team on *University Challenge*, where they eventually lost to Balliol after Clive blurted out the wrong answer to a straightforward tie-breaker question about Verdi, and began work on his eternally uncompleted PhD thesis about Dante's influence on Shelley. For half a century, Cambridge, with its colleges and bookshops, traditions and snobberies, students and eccentrics, its punts and cafes, milling tourists and speeding cyclists, has been the place Clive has always come back to.

In recent years, when his health still allowed it, he would make a slow beeline for the secondhand book stall in the market square run by the taciturn Hugh Harding, who would scour the car boot sales of Cambridgeshire for the unwanted libraries of deceased enthusiasts and scholars and proudly lay out his finds every Tuesday and Thursday. Hugh's bookstall ('one of the greatest bookshops on earth') exercised an endless fascination. Every few months, Clive would purge his bookshelves, disposing of hundreds of books that, common sense told him, he would never get round to reading again. And every few weeks he would limp the half-mile into town and return, against his better judgement, lugging a bag bulging with new discoveries unearthed at Hugh's.

'As I was scheduled to die off myself, even if I did not precisely know when, it was madness to start making small piles of books on Hugh's stall that I wanted to take home,' he wrote in one of the essays in *Latest Readings*. 'But the madness was divine. Somewhere in there was an itching sense of duty. The childish urge to understand everything doesn't necessarily fade when the time approaches for you to do the most adult thing of all: vanish.'

That 'childish urge to understand everything' is arguably the key to Clive's whole kaleidoscopic career, from the nosy curiosity of his television interviews to the self-scrutiny of his later poems and the ambitious breadth of his greatest literary monument, the vast and idiosyncratic survey of Western civilisation that's packed into the 850-page *Cultural Amnesia*. Writing, after all, is never really about what you know. It's a process of discovery, the ultimate mechanism for finding out what you think and what you have come to understand. The raw material may come from books, from conversations or from the experience of living, but it is not until you try to shape and capture it in words that you really know what you have learned about the world.

For Clive, with his voracious appetite for reading and his prehensile memory for detail, what goes in once stays there for ever. Unlike the rest of us, he seems to be able to gouge and google whatever he needs from the deepest recesses of his brain, immediately and selectively, finding not just the *mot juste* but the *idée juste* with unhesitating precision. That's the secret of his fast-talking, fast-writing talent, and the key to his ability, even now, to write a thousand words of tight, persuasive and relevant text in the time most of us would take to creep down to the bottom of the first page. Nothing is forgotten. Nothing is ever lost. It's as if every book he's ever read is there on the shelf, at his fingertips, all the time.

As a reader and buyer of books, Clive is in his element in Cambridge. Apart from Hugh's and the other bookstalls in the market, he has haunted the Oxfam shops in search of unexpected treasures. And he has spent days of his life in the city's two mainstream bookshops, Heffers in Trinity Street and Waterstones. Heffers is a Cambridge landmark, huge, comprehensive, founded in 1876 and proudly independent in its approach, though it was eventually taken over by its Oxford equivalent, Blackwell's, in 1999. Its local rival is Waterstones, in Sidney Street, part of a 300-shop chain, but crammed with the specialist titles and delightful obscurities required to meet the needs of a demanding community of readers and academics.

The two shops, Heffers and Waterstones, are both honoured, even-handedly, in one of the most engaging poems in *Injury Time*, 'Apotheosis at the Signing Table'. This predicts a final scene in which Clive, on his last legs, staggers into town to do his duty, for one last time, to the book trade. Flourishing his svelte-tipped pen, he signs the pile of books placed before him 'for hours on end' before collapsing, 'croaking tragically' (and punning shamelessly) and passing on to the great bookshop in the sky. It's a charming scene, beautifully sketched in classic rhymed iambic pentameters, with some lovely touches of knowing and self-deprecating irony. No-one's expecting him, so he stands, at first, 'with a long-practised half-lost look / Somewhere beside the stack of my new book', waiting to be approached and persuaded to donate his autograph. When he's asked to sign, he sits down slowly, 'seemingly paralysed / By sheer humility', as the bookshop staff bring him piles of volumes he can't remember ever having written – though if you believe that, you'll believe anything.

While Clive has always been a great buyer of books, he has been a great seller of them, too. In a bookshop that may stock anything from 30000 to 60000 titles, there will only be a few hundred that sell in any quantity. The few that sell subsidise the many that don't, and Clive's books, from the perennially bestselling *Unreliable Memoirs* to unexpected hits like *Play All*, his recent survey of the world of the television series box set, have helped keep the lights on in many a bookshop over the years. His gift for self-promotion and his readiness to take part in media interviews, signings and other marketing activities have benefited retailers and publishers alike, making him not just a popular author but also one of the few profitable poets of modern times.

The important question about 'Apotheosis at the Signing Table' is why this brief, insubstantial, one-joke poem seems to work so well. There's nothing particularly remarkable about its form, except for the slight soft-shoe shuffle at the turning point, eight lines in, where he starts to go downhill and the regular couplets are momentarily pushed apart, so that successive lines rhyme 'stock', 'sign', 'by-line', 'clock'. But the content, though fanciful, is entirely consistent with the Clive James we have known for all these years.

This is not a narrator talking. This is the Clive we are familiar with – the flip, witty Clive who revolutionised TV criticism, the humorously autobiographical Clive of the *Unreliable Memoirs*, the Clive we saw as a television performer, alternately self-aggrandising and self-effacing, the serious, bookish Clive of the essays and lit-crit reviews, the poet, the Cambridge resident, the unstoppable invalid, the man himself. The voice is a voice we know. The attitude is familiar, too. He's talking about death – his death – and he's playing it for laughs, going down with a pun.

We've seen him hold up the skull and address it from many different angles in the other poems in *Sentenced to Life* and *Injury*

Time, powerfully evoking loss and regret, pain and resignation. But here we feel the authenticity, even down to the vanity of wishing to be remembered, in death, as a man inseparable from the books that surround him. 'Heffers or Waterstones, this is goodbye / But I rejoice that I came here to die'. There is humour here, to the last, in his stubborn refusal to choose which of the two bookshops to grace with his passing. And there is something genuinely stately and poignant about those last four lines. The final joke – 'This is where he signed his life away' – evokes echoes of 'He who lives by the sword dies by the sword', which is ultimately derived from the teaching of Jesus, as reported in Matthew's gospel. But in view of Clive's teasing comments about his publisher's concern to see him fulfil his contract and complete the final volume of his memoirs before he hands in his dinner pail, he may also have been thinking of the idea of signing one's life away in quite a different context.

The poem works because the initial idea is very Clive James – quirky, unexpected and original – and its execution, including the carefully paced build-up to the punchline, is a neat encapsulation of many of the characteristics we recognise in him and his poetry.

'Apotheosis at the Signing Table' is, you'll probably agree, a terrible title. (It's not his worst – he once wrote a superb song with Pete Atkin about the end of the Flower Power era and then condemned it to perpetual obscurity by calling it 'An Array of Passionate Lovers', which meant nothing to anybody and didn't even link up very closely with anything in the lyrics.) I thought I knew what 'apotheosis' meant – a peak or culmination or crowning moment. But I had to look it up to be sure, and now I'm worried about the other dictionary definition I found ('deification; the elevation of someone to divine status') and wondering whether there is supposed to be some sort of double meaning going on here. If there is, I'm not getting it. I'd have been more comfortable with just 'The Signing Table', without the apotheosis, but it's Clive's creation, so it's his choice.

There's also one unexplained joke, which will not be obvious to many people outside the book trade, hidden just beneath the surface of this poem. Bookshops like to be able to offer copies that have been signed by the author, because their customers like and value them. But smart authors are only too willing to oblige, for a reason of their own. Books are sold in to the bookshops by publishers on a sale or return basis. If the book goes out to the shop but remains unsold after a few months, it will be returned to the publisher, who then has to refund the money paid for it. A signed copy, however, cannot be returned. So once it has been signed, the book is as good as sold, however long it may hang around on the shelves. In autographing a big pile of books before he keels over in Waterstones or Heffers, whichever it is, the dying poet is showing his worldly nous by guaranteeing just a few more definite sales and a few more pounds in royalties for the benefit of his heirs and assigns.

Apotheosis at the Signing Table

Looking ahead for places to sit down,
Come spring I might, one last time, limp downtown
And into Heffers, into Waterstones,
In either order, haul my creaking bones,

To stand, with a long-practised half-lost look,
Somewhere beside the stack of my new book
Until I'm asked to sign. As if surprised
I'll sit down, slowly, seeming paralysed
By sheer humility as they bring stock
Of books that I forgot I wrote. I'll sign
Each tempting title-page with my by-line
Like a machine for hours on end. The clock
Will seem not to exist. My signature
Will grow, however, steadily less sure,
Until, the felt-tip quivering in my grasp,
I scrawl the hieroglyphs of my last gasp.
A final short sip from my cup of tea
And I will topple, croaking tragically.
Slumped on the carpet, I will look around,
And all the walls of books in the background,
More splendid even than they were before,
Will seem to hear my small voice from the floor.
'Heffers or Waterstones, this is goodbye,
But I rejoice that I came here to die,
So one day those who know my books may say
That this is where he signed his life away.'

21

'I'm Not Going to Go Out
and Ride My Bike'

Cambridge, September 2018. A small party at Clive's house, organised by his publisher, Picador, and hosted by his daughter, Claerwen, to mark the launch of his epic poem, *The River in the Sky*. Just a handful of friends and a few publishing people, with no press and PR hype. Tom Stoppard, at eighty-one, still tall, mop-haired and impossibly charismatic, slipping away into the Japanese-mapleless garden every few minutes to smoke a cigarette. The brilliant Julian Barnes, genial, self-effacing, describing himself as 'one of the listeners'. 'You always need listeners,' says Clive. 'Julian was a listener, while Amis and I talked nonstop.' John Carey and his wife, Gill, twinkling, bright, interesting and interested. Pete Atkin, Clive's collaborator in a wonderful fifty-year songwriting partnership, amiably mingling, resigned to the fact that this side of his chum's talent seems doomed to be neglected for ever. Mary Beard, laughing, curious, full of enthusiasm and stories. Don Paterson and the *TLS*'s Alan Jenkins, both modestly playing down their roles as editors in helping Clive hone and polish his poems. 'He does hit bum notes,' Paterson, the musician, concedes. 'But look what you get when he gets it right.

He gives you brilliant moments.' And Clive's wife, Prue, happy, proud, protective, at his side as he signs copies of the book for these ageing members of a golden generation. There's a lot of love in the room, and a lot of energy, as well as talent. Common sense tells you that this world can't go on for ever, but it's hard to believe it won't.

Clive himself is in good spirits. He looks battered, as always these days, and he's smaller than he used to be. But the spark is still there and his voice is stronger than the last few times I've seen him. He talks about *The River in the Sky* as if it's the final summing-up of his poetic career, and then immediately goes on to threaten us with *River in the Sky, Vol 2*.

'Now it's out, I keep thinking of more things I should have put in,' he says. 'Watch this space.'

He is already halfway through writing the sixth volume of his *Unreliable Memoirs* and he is not allowed to stop writing that for any reason ('No excuses accepted, not even mortality'). Picador has him under contract and the publishers won't take no for an answer. Surely there's no time for more epic poetry?

'I'm not making any promises' he grins, '– either way.'

Tom Stoppard, who says that it was Clive's literary criticism ('a real voice – like some bloke talking with a drink in his hand') that made him start reading contemporary poetry for the first time, recalls the early days of Clive's illness, when he collapsed in New York. It was 2010. Clive had, as he puts it, 'already died a couple of times that year'. He was far too frail to fly, but by the time the *Queen Mary 2* docked he was suffering from deep vein thrombosis and was rushed to Manhattan's Mount Sinai Hospital. It took the doctors ten days to drag him back from the edge.

'I called you, Prue, because someone had told me Clive was desperately ill,' Stoppard remembers. 'But I wouldn't have bothered if I'd thought I'd be seeing him celebrating a book launch in Cambridge eight years later.'

Don Paterson gives a short, informal speech. He has been working with Clive for more than two years to knock *The River in the Sky* into shape and he knows the text better than anyone. Together, they have taken the elements of a lifetime – the things Clive has experienced, the things he's enjoyed, the flashes of insight, the memories of people and places – and moulded them into a vast poetic autobiography that has its own internal logic.

At first sight, Paterson admits, it seems almost shapeless. But gradually themes and motifs emerge, threading themselves through the narrative, recurring in different forms and unexpected contexts. Light plays a key role, with twinkling stars, glinting diodes, glittering chrome, glistening dew-drops, shining mirrors and 'beams of colour in the sunlight' illuminating scene after scene, as the narrative dances through time and space. Episodes from Clive's Aussie childhood rub shoulders with images of Ancient Egypt and modern Cambridge and treasured glimpses of Africa and South America, Hawaii and the Himalayas, Japan and Antarctica and all the other places his globetrotting career has taken him to. Clive may be heading towards the darkness of oblivion, but his memories are bright and clear. Here, surrounded by those he has loved and worked with for the best part of a lifetime, his restless spirit is home at last.

As we raise our glasses to drink Clive's health, I look around and realise that within this room, packed with literary and critical talent, I am in a privileged position. Because I'm working on this book, I am one of the handful of people who have been given the opportunity to read the poem in advance. Don Paterson has been intimately implicated in the project for many months. Tom Stoppard has been involved, commenting and making suggestions, since the earliest drafts. One or two others have had early glimpses of the manuscript. But most of the rest, even Clive's oldest friends, are just getting their hands on *The River in the Sky* for the first time. I wonder what they will make of it.

First, I imagine, they may feel some sense of bafflement, even perhaps resentment, at the sheer scale of the enterprise. It's not like another slim volume of short lyric verses. A 122-page poem makes an immediate demand for commitment. You can't just dip into it. You have to be prepared to start at the beginning and give it hours of focused attention, to allow the flow and structure a chance to unfold, to grant the themes time to emerge and develop. The literary giants around me will have more experience than I have of squaring up to epic poetic works and approaching them with the appropriate levels of concentration and receptivity. But I know that my first reading of the text was nothing more than a beginning. I certainly found it too much to take in, and I seriously underestimated the links and shaping forces that hold the elements of the poem together. It was only on the second or third run through that the essential coherence of the material began to establish itself in my mind. It took time for me to start to understand why Clive had chosen to take on the challenge of trying to wrestle his original sheaf of unfinished poems – a 'small stack of would-be poetic fragments', he called it in the *Guardian* – into a single, all-embracing epic.

So how will the friends who are here today, and the wider public, react to *The River in the Sky*? Clive's been talking to the press about it recently and he certainly wants it to be read and enjoyed – and not just as a valedictory message.

'I want people to read it,' he told the *New Statesman*. 'If you want people not to be able to stop reading, you've got to keep the pace up, even in the slow bits. Watch the tango dancers doing hesitation step and you'll see they never really stop.'

As if to underline the message that this is not the end of the line, he gave the *New Statesman* a new poem just a couple of weeks before this launch party for *The River in the Sky*. Its key lines – 'And I am in two minds: all set to go, / Mad keen to stay' – sum up exactly what we are seeing here in the little house in Cambridge. Clive has effectively packed his bags for the last departure. He has come to terms with his failures and regrets, renewed and strengthened the ties with his nearest and dearest and written his own epitaph many times over in poems and prose over these last few years of his slow decline. But while he waits for his flight to be called, his zest for life and enthusiasm for work are feeding an extraordinary and prolonged burst of productivity.

A few hours after we say goodbye to Clive, he is on BBC2's *Front Row Late*, being interviewed by Mary Beard. What's the secret, she asks him, of his prolific output since becoming terminally ill?

'Here's the big thing. You're not doing anything else,' Clive replies. 'What else am I going to do? I'm not going to go out and ride my bike.'

Acknowledgements

The idea for this book originated in a casual conversation with Clive shortly after I had finished writing *Loose Canon*, my book about the marvellous songs he had written with his old friend Pete Atkin. Clive asked me what I was going to write next. When I tentatively mentioned the possibility of a follow-up volume about his poems, he sounded positive. When the subject came up again, he egged me on. Two hints is quite enough for me. So this is all his fault.

I'd known Clive and Pete and their songs since the 1970s, so in writing *Loose Canon*, I knew what I was talking about. But this would be different. Apart from my delight in the way Clive uses words and my fondness for the handful of his poems I already knew, the main attraction of the idea was that no-one else had done it. The idea may have appealed to him for exactly the same reason. He had enjoyed the meandering, speculative, digressionary style that had evolved during the writing of the earlier book, and I had enjoyed the lazy, gossipy afternoon sessions at his house in Cambridge that passed for research interviews.

Once the idea for this book had gelled into a concept and the concept had hardened into a project, I went away and wrote the chapter about 'Asma Unpacks Her Pretty Clothes', just to see if I could make it work. It seemed easy, because the elements were all to hand.

There was a powerful, well-made poem from Clive, the glamorous, dangerous figure of Bashar al-Assad's wife in the foreground and an interesting background story about *Vogue* journalist Joan Juliet Buck's valiant attempts to convey a small part of the truth about Syria, despite the best efforts of the magazine's editors and senior managers.

But the next chapter I tackled, about the delicate art of editing, brought me face to face with my broad and profound ignorance about the details of the subject. I'd read a fair amount of poetry while studying English at the University of York, but that was a long time ago (so long, in fact, that I'd sat through several spectacularly dull lectures from FR Leavis). I went to Edinburgh for a brief meeting with the gruff but kindly Don Paterson, Clive's long-time editor and a brilliant poet in his own right, and came back with my head full of ideas and a clear understanding that I was going to have to read an awful lot of poetry and criticism over the next few months. In fact, the whole process took two years, but without Don's informed and provocative contribution, it would certainly never have got started. He is a recurring presence in this book, even – especially – in the many sections where I have gone back and crossed out his name in the ignoble hope of passing the good ideas off as my own.

I'm grateful to Clive for his time, his conversation, his encouragement and his poems. I'm grateful to Don for his spiky wisdom, to Pete Atkin for his measured, thoughtful comments on each new draft chapter, to Robin Bynoe for his invigorating criticisms, and to Kate and Sarah Penning, Sarah Burton and my daughter, Zoë, and son, Nick, for their support as members of the 'first readers' team.

While mentioning my kids, I should assure them – and anyone else who's interested – that my centenarian great-grandmother (and hence their great-great-grandmother), who features with such unlikely and convenient synchronicity in the chapter about Clive's poem 'Six Degrees of Separation from Shelley', really did exist. Eleanor Parkman was indeed born in 1859, and she did tell me about her own grandma remembering the horsemen bringing the news of the Battle of Waterloo. It's never occurred to me before, but if she were alive now Gran would be 160.

I would like to thank all those who took the time to read the advance proof copies of *So Brightly* and send me their thoughts, including, in particular, John Carey, Stephen Fry, Stuart Maconie, Philip Collins, Stephen Edgar, Peter Goldsworthy, David Free, Christian Wiman, Sam Leith, Joan Juliet Buck and Jo Crocker.

My thanks are due, too, to Gary Dexter, who allowed me to pinch many of the best jokes and insights from his fine book, *The People's Favourite Poems*, to the ever-positive Francesca Eden, to Isabel Rogers for permission to quote from her excellent blog interview with Don Paterson and to Marcia Adams Ho for her graphic skills and flexibility.

As always, I'm indebted for all kinds of publishing advice and guidance to Clare Christian, a collaborator now for twenty-one years, on and off, and to her RedDoor colleagues, Heather Boisseau and Anna Burtt. My other professional mentor, new to my career but not to Clive's, is the superb publicist Jacqui Graham.

Thank you all. This feels like the beginning of something good. What do you see when you turn *on* the light? I can't tell you, but I know it's mine.

Index

Also by Ian Shircore

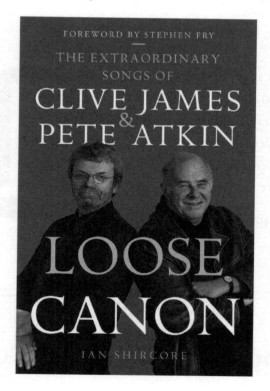

FOREWORD BY STEPHEN FRY

THE EXTRAORDINARY SONGS OF

CLIVE JAMES & PETE ATKIN

LOOSE CANON

IAN SHIRCORE

The fascinating story of the little-known but wonderful songs of Clive James and Pete Atkin

'In these wonderful songs - timeless and yet so achingly redolent of a time - the tough, smart, tender elegance of Clive Jame's intellect and lyricism found its perfect home in the subtle, graceful arms of Pete Atkin's settings'
Stuart Maconie

SCAN HERE TO LISTEN TO A SAMPLE TRACK

Find out more about RedDoor
Press and sign up to our
newsletter to hear about our
latest releases, author events,
exciting **competitions**
and more at

reddoorpress.co.uk

YOU CAN ALSO FOLLOW US:

  @RedDoorBooks

  RedDoor

  @RedDoorBooks